Inner Voice Revolution

Redesigning Self-Talk for Personal Growth & Decision-Making

Joshua Smalley

ISBN ~ 979-8-9920390-0-9

Table of Contents

Dedication

This book is dedicated to my parents, who instilled a sense of self-awareness and a desire for personal growth. Strategies such as those discussed in this book are a direct result of my parents modeling consistent pursuit of meaning in life.

~~~

Additionally, I dedicate this book to my wife, who is an immense support. She models how to refine, polish, and craft ideas in a way that others can understand and appreciate. With the help of her wisdom, input, and general support, I composed my ideas and shared them with the world.

~~~

Finally, I dedicate this book to my children. A bright future is my hope for each of them. I hope they will leave a positive imprint on the world. In these hopes, I find motivation to share this book and contribute to the collective health and maturation of everyone.

Chapter 1:

Inner Voice

Everyone who wills can hear the inner voice. It is within everyone. -Mahatma Gandhi

Life is full of difficulty and confusion, and decisions seem to grow in complexity as you age. Often, we are people who are lost and grasping for answers, whether those be the significant questions of life or everyday decisions. What our values should be, how to navigate relationships, and what career move makes sense all descend upon us as we steer our lives. So many voices cloud our minds. Family, friends, co-workers, and even the neighbors get their two cents in from time to time. Often, ideas conflict with each other, and we find ourselves in doubt, uncertain, and stuck. Sometimes, we need external advice, but sometimes, those voices can be all too overwhelming.

What about your own voice? If you are like anyone else, your own voice can be confusing, too. You probably live a dynamic life. In other words, you are not a static person. What you think, know, value, enjoy, and believe today may, and likely will, change to varying degrees in the future. Think back to your 15-year-old self. Do you think the same? Do you know the same things? Do you value all the same things? Do you enjoy all the same things? Do you hold all the same beliefs you held when you were 15?

You share some similarities with your 15-year-old self, no doubt, but if you break it down, the changes in your thinking and values may surprise you. What you think and believe changes over time and can cast doubt on the reliability of your own inner thoughts. Fluidity remains a central hallmark and natural process of the human experience. This fluidity is a testament to our open-mindedness and growth mindsets; it is a cardinal difference between us and other living beings on this planet.

What if the secret to success in navigating life's challenges was hidden inside you all along? What if there was a way to tap into your inner voice and find the wisdom and direction needed to establish your values and make difficult decisions?

The Hologram Conversation provides a solution. It is a unique strategy that uses your inner voice for personal growth and better decision-making. These Hologram Conversations offer a unique framework for accessing clarity amid life's challenges, reducing confusion and uncertainty. Furthermore, you will find that these conversations help solidify your values and general direction in life, offering heightened hope and purpose in uncertain times.

In short, Hologram Conversations offer you a new pathway for discovering and confirming your life's direction.

The Inner Voice

Do you talk to yourself? Do you ever sense that internal monologue that runs like a constant hum in the background of your mind? Even as you begin this book, in this very moment, quiet and inner thoughts emerge. You might be wondering about the questions posed within this paragraph, reflecting on the quote at the beginning of the chapter, or wandering off on the to-do list for today.

For better or for worse, we face the reality of this inner voice every day. A private, silent conversation occurs in our minds. It may be a single voice, or it may develop into a full dialogue with multiple voices in our minds. In fact, for many, it may feel like multiple personas speaking their perspectives simultaneously.

An idea suddenly makes an appearance in the mind, and a response subsequently emerges. This is followed by yet another voice, and then another thought, and so on throughout the day. As the inner voice continues to navigate the day, competing ideas may come to your attention, and before you know it, you find yourself arguing with yourself. The realization arrives in your consciousness that you have, unintentionally, been carrying out a full debate in your mind.

Sometimes, this inner voice presents itself as a clear back-and-forth argument toward a pending decision. At other times, it may reveal itself as a random wandering across a plane of ideas. Sometimes, it remains precise and calculated. Other times this inner voice finds itself unregulated, chaotic, and unpredictable, randomly reaching about at topics like a child in a candy shop.

Beyond these binary options presented, a sea of possible other types of internal thoughts may pervade our minds. We may be quite conscious and wandering. We might be allowing our thoughts to float, all while coming to clear conclusions about ideas in life. We may be daydreaming and listening to the inner voice, but for recreational purposes only, dismissing any real gravitas such juvenile voice might hold in our lives.

Sometimes, the voice is more obvious, and we remain conscious of it, while other times, it runs in the background, undetected and seemingly unguided. Thus, the internal voice operates continuously, in a variety of forms and roles, in our minds.

This voice goes by any number of titles, some importing a sense of morality into the concept of an internal voice. Some titles also imply more sporadic moments of inner thoughts as opposed to a constant inner conversation. Some of these labels are inner monologue, inner dialogue, the voice inside your head, inner critic, self-talk, gut, premonition, inner guide, moral guide, moral compass, conscience, the voice within, and intuition. We will use "inner voice" as a label for this human experience.

This inner voice is an important part of our everyday lives. Sometimes, it is healthy, while at other times, it can be unhealthy. Sometimes, it is neither, or even a hybrid of both. Some people use the inner voice as a source of motivation, inspiration, or encouragement. Some utilize the voice through meditation.

This voice, whatever the value we place upon it or how we use it, governs our day-to-day thinking. It has been identified and explored across time and cultures, even seen in modernity through memes like the age-old devil on one shoulder and angel on the other. Ultimately, whatever this internal voice is, a clear element of this voice is that it is common to the human experience, universal in its presence in human beings.

As previously remarked, our inner voice often exists as a subconscious force. It can be intentional, but it mostly lives and moves under the surface of our conscious selves.

We are in line at the grocery store, we see something and then an internal monologue kicks in and runs on its own script. We begin a monologue, internally, about something or someone pestering us. The kid throws a tantrum in front of us, and we start imagining how we would parent the child.

The checkout staff member moves too slowly, and you imagine all the zingers you can shout at him.

Maybe you notice some misplaced items on the shelf, and you wonder how such employees keep their jobs.

On the other hand, maybe your thoughts wander positively. You notice the person in front of you is beautiful. Your mind whisks you, rapidly, across full-speed imaginary memories, through a 40-year life with this person chock-full of travel, adventure, children, and retirement.

Maybe you see the effort the checkout staff member offers, and you wonder what motivates her and what beautiful moments and memories fill her mind.

Maybe you see a child giggling with a parent, and you cherish the image of pure, unadulterated humanity in its purest form.

Whatever the thoughts in the checkout line, we find ourselves lost in our minds and unaware that we are lost. This is not intended as a judgment claim; it is only an objective description that may reflect many of our daily realities.

We have an inner voice, and it seems impossible to hold the reins at all times. This inner voice thrusts us forward into ideas, imaginations, wonderings, and limitations before we grow conscious of its activity. We go about most of our days in a type of reactionary mode with the internal voice piloting according to its own pleasure.

A history of extensive research has explored self-talk, affirmations, mindfulness, mantras, word-specific meditation, and more. Meta-analyses exist from many researchers. Thousands of research papers include varying sample sizes and a wide range of methodologies. Many studies speak to self-talk that acts as a self-regulatory mechanism. Some research even suggests that positive self-talk impacts the chemistry of the brain.

Countless findings point to the power of our inner voice. The research is clear that this inner voice can be a tool for personal growth, self-management, mindfulness, happiness, and a sense of meaning.

The opposite of each of these can also be true, underscoring the importance and power of this internal voice. Research points to how it can serve as a detriment to one's life. If a person fails to manage or cultivate the inner voice, personal struggles may ensue. From depression, anxiety, psychosis, loss of meaning, or a loss of personal efficacy, the inner voice gone unchecked may lead to a dark path.

While not all research is created equal, and some shortcomings in the quality of research for positive self-talk research are documented, the preponderance of evidence seems to point to the value of maintaining a positive inner voice.

As a result of this tradition of research, people's lived experiences, and years of philosophical ruminations on the topic, a massive collection of self-help books, essays, articles, films, poems, songs, art, podcasts, and conferences have emerged. These are aimed at coaching people to develop their positive self-talk. A whole new self-help industry, specific to cultivating one's inner voice, exists and is growing.

Other fields of human development and thriving explore the importance of the inner voice. Meditation practices incorporate an awareness of the internal voice. Letting go of external influences on the mind and learning to listen to and observe the thoughts occurring within your mind are fundamental meditative practices.

Furthermore, life coaches and counselors frequently discuss this topic. Life coaches, counselors, psychologists, therapists, and gurus often recommend self-affirmations, positive self-talk, or a positive frame of mind. Experts recommend using morning routines that contain self-affirmations. They argue that positive self-talk is part and parcel of a healthy mind and a healthy life. Clearly, the inner voice has power.

What if we took back some control of this inner voice and used it to our advantage?

What if we made this voice more conscious? What if we were slightly more intentional with this voice at strategic times?

What if we could invite a full range of our voices into a conversation to think through ideas?

What if we could tap into future wisdom by using some inner voice creativity?

More specifically, and in the spirit of this book, how would our daily lives be impacted if we used our current inner voice to consult the voices of our future selves?

~~~

From the nature of these questions, you might wonder if your inner voice is about to be stifled, confined, or manipulated somehow. Is your inner voice persona screaming for freedom already? Do you hear its objections to those questions?

To alleviate your inner voice's fears, this book will not hijack your everyday mindless or mindful wanderings and daydreams. If you revel in your checkout line wanderings, you should be happy to know that you may keep them and indulge them. The voice inside needs time and space to breathe, to ebb and flow unimpeded. We cannot be in direct control over every internal thought and thereby cause extreme mental fatigue.

Think of this book's work as an additive element to your inner voice. You learn to better leverage that inner voice to have high-impact conversations that will, inevitably, provide direction in life. You will explore some aspects of your life left completely or loosely unexamined. You will become strategically intentional at strategic times to use your inner voice as a personal ally for wisdom, guidance, planning, exploration, and self-discovery. As this new method of self-discovery will be about creating clarity, understanding, and direction in life, it will be a creative process in the purest sense.

We will define this creative process, which we call a **"Hologram Conversation,"** as a brief introduction before a more in-depth breakdown.

Hologram Conversations are a framework for seeking wisdom and direction in life through imaginative and explorative dialogues with future versions of yourself.

Or put in another, more concise, way:

Hologram Conversations seek advice and wisdom through an imaginative dialogue with yourself.

It should be noted that there is a purposeful shift from "inner voice" to "dialogues." A Hologram Conversation will be a conversation that requires you to speak with the inner voices of your current self and your imagined future selves. Therefore, it is a dialogue, not just a singular voice. From this point on, the "inner voices" will be used to combine into "dialogues" and these dialogues are the foundation of "Hologram Conversations."

Chapter 2:

Hologram Conversations Breakdown

Always listen to your inner voice. –Oprah Winfrey

Revisiting a concept from the previous chapter will help us move forward in this chapter. We are fluid people who change over time. Our thinking, behaviors, and beliefs change to some degree. As a result, our current inner voice may not be the best voice for consultation.

If your future self will change over time, might it be interesting to access the wisdom of your future self? It might even be interesting to speak to your future self at different stages of life. By listening to your voice across time, you might gain a clearer understanding of yourself and the direction you want for your life.

Imagine your 18-year-old self engaging in a serious sit-down conversation with your 30-year-old self. If only, right? If only your future self could have corralled the wildness of your youth? Or maybe the opposite is true: if only my lustful and passionate youth could speak some wisdom into my stagnated elder self.

So, imagine your 30-year-old self being consulted by the wisdom and learning of your 60-year-old self and vice versa. Imagine how the wisdom, insight, tips, counseling, encouragement, and warnings gleaned from one's future self could act as a guide throughout life. Imagine how your current, more youthful self might also push back and inspire your future self.

Hindsight is 20/20, they say. The wisdom, thinking, and values of your future self might serve to steady your current life's actions and values. If only such a conversation were possible. If only we could teleport through time and go back and forth with our previous and future selves to help perfect who we are in the present.

It is with this understanding of our ever-changing state as humans, coupled with the imaginative possibilities of consulting one's future self, that we can introduce Hologram Conversations. Indeed, with a bit of creativity, we can engage in a conversation previously thought impossible. Maybe we can traverse time and seek the wisdom of our youth and old age.

The goal of a Hologram Conversation is to combine our potential for change with the imagined insights from our future selves. Through an imaginative process, these conversations seek to understand the unique and diverse perspectives held by our future selves in order to steer our current lives. We can talk to our future selves to figure out what we want to do with our lives in the present day.

What is a Hologram Conversation?

Let us remember the definition from Chapter 1:

Hologram Conversations are a framework for seeking wisdom and direction in life through imaginative and explorative dialogues with future versions of yourself.

What does this mean, exactly? Specifically, a Hologram Conversation is an imaginary conversation with at least three future, imagined versions of yourself. Your inner voice is used to embody these three future selves. These selves then engage in a structured conversation with your current inner voice. The whole process is intentional and strategically timed to glean useful insight and direction in your personal life.

To add clarity, let us examine what a Hologram Conversation would look like. If someone were to walk in on me during one of my conversations, here is what they would see:

I am sitting down at my dinner table. It is the evening, and everything is quiet and still in my house. The lights are turned off to help me concentrate. My family has gone into town to enjoy an evening out, and I am alone. I begin speaking out loud, although sometimes I do these conversations silently. It looks as if I am speaking to people at the table even though no one is there in reality.

To the objective viewer, it might seem odd. Ideas about an important upcoming decision are being shared out loud. There are pauses in silence. And then, there are sudden audible statements from me as if I am responding to someone's ideas at the table. It looks like I am having a passionate, but calm, argument with myself.

This cycle goes on for some time and repeats itself many times—the speaking of ideas followed by moments of silence. After approximately 30 minutes, I state a final conclusion; it appears to the onlooker in between a reasonable path forward has been forged for the upcoming decision discussed. Also, I offer "thank you" statements to other vacant seats at the table. You would see me breathe deeply a few times and meditate for a few minutes. My eyes are closed. There is a slight smile, and a sense of acceptance shows on my face. You might wonder if I am crazy, but you could not deny the look of peace across my body and the reasonable conclusion reached at the end of the discussion.

This is what you would see if you saw the Hologram Conversation live. It would be the CCTV version. Likely, you would be left wondering what just happened. It seemed substantive, but it also appeared bizarre.

Prior to breaking down Hologram Conversations into specific steps in future chapters, we can understand some general aspects of these conversations.

Hologram Conversations are a kind of mind game or thought experiment. In a Hologram Conversation, you sit down at a strategic location, like at a kitchen table, and imagine your future selves sitting, like holograms, at the other vacant chairs at the table. The location itself will be discussed in further detail, but the point is to have a comfortable space that is private and will facilitate your concentration on the conversation.

You now imagine your future selves, and they will all be from different ages across your lifetime to represent different perspectives over time. Once you have those three individuals in mind (maybe your 40-year-old self, 60-year-old self, and 80-year-old self), you can use your imagination to make them suddenly appear before you in your "mind's eye." You can materialize them with clothing, skin, wrinkles, facial expressions, aches and pains, smiles and chuckles. The whole version of each future self is imagined and animated in your mind's eye.

You can also imagine your future selves in a more animated fashion, like a video game environment, with your future avatars facing you. With these three older versions of yourself "present," you can focus on having a conversation with each of them, no matter how realistic or cartoonish they may be visually represented. The Hologram Conversation, at this point, narrows in on the goal of gaining insight and wisdom into your life's current situations, questions, challenges, and contexts. There will be a protocol to guide the conversation meaningfully.

On the point of three different future versions of yourself across time, a range of ages offers unique perspectives. Your future selves, in a Hologram Conversation, will likely contribute from different angles, experiences, knowledge, and motivations. Depending on the content of your own Hologram Conversations, these future selves may discuss with you your current values, direction, goals, dreams, relationships, career, hobbies, and more. They will come to the table with different understandings about these aspects of life. A career, for example, is seen quite differently at age eighty than it is at age twenty. The same is true for relationships. You will want a range of perspectives to avoid the echo chamber of just the elderly, 80-year-old's advice. It will be good advice, no doubt, but it should not be the only advice you seek. Your 40-year-old self has something similarly meaningful on the same topics.

During the conversation, your future selves will shed light on your current challenges and victories. Because they offer diverse perspectives, you will see your current affairs in the broader context of your life over time. It will help prioritize your current life and understand them in a bigger context than merely the "here and now." Observing yourself over time also affords you the opportunity to see your changes. This process can help you understand your values and passions as they evolve over time. Hologram Conversations are a window into your personal evolution while providing clarity about your current state in life.

In some ways, it is as if your life opens up like a book before your mind's eye. Consequently, you gain clarity into how the current chapters of your life fit into the overall picture of your life and legacy. Think of this as a simultaneous expanding and contracting understanding of self.

Importantly, Hologram Conversations make use of significant assumptions. It is a mental exercise, so a bit of a creative license is required. You have to imagine who your future selves are in all their grandeur and all their banality. An initial objection to the "fantasy world" of this exercise might be that you have no clue about your current self, let alone your future self or selves. You might feel it preposterous to imagine anything substantive about yourself in the future, especially when life at present may be unclear at best and tragic at worst. Hologram Conversations ask you, who is currently unclear about some things in life, to hold insights into what the future holds for you. And somehow, you will gain wisdom from these imagined future selves? How?

First, we should examine our use of escape. Often, we need to escape our daily situations and take a breath of air to regain our composure and our mental wellness. This is the utility of rest, vacations, exercise, brain breaks, seasonal breaks, gap years, sabbaticals, and more. It is our use of movies, books, date nights, and parties. When deep inside a project, life challenge, or daily rut, an occasional break from reality provides needed recharging. You return to the project somewhat fresh and with new perspectives or at least renewed energy to take on life's challenges.

Accordingly, Hologram Conversations can function similarly as a necessary escape to gain perspective and rest. These conversations can temporarily break from the rut of life in order to broaden your perspective. The urgency of now and what you happen to be facing is spread out across the trajectory of your entire life. You gain, in these conversations, invaluable perspectives that help frame and contextualize your current life and critical decisions. Your current moments and experiences deserve their proper place in the "chapters" of your life. Hologram Conversations help you arrive at these understandings.

There is a second aspect to this as well. Often, I speak to individuals who are in the middle of a challenging moment. I simply ask them what their future self will think about this current situation 30 years from now. Will this moment be remembered? Will the current situation have any bearing on that future self? Will that future self who is driving that car across town 30 years from now even remember this current moment? This reduces the person's anxiety in many cases. It re-centers them. Even if exceedingly urgent, the current moment is placed into a more appropriate perspective and understood more for what it is—a moment in a lifetime, good or bad. Perspective that reaches beyond the quicksand of now can help uproot you from the chaos, uncertainty, and immobility of your current state.

Even if your projections into the future are incorrect and you imagine future selves that do not comport with reality, the exercise alone may help you begin to lift your eyes up to gain perspective across time for your current situations. It is the tried and true "forest for the trees" adage.

Of course, you may not be in crisis and wonder if Hologram Conversations are necessary. Crisis is relative. Everyone is going through something, good, bad, and in between. Hologram Conversations afford wisdom and insight no matter the current plight, or lack thereof, of your life. Perspective-taking proves valuable no matter the severity, victorious, or unimportant elements of life.

Think of it as going to the movies for your mind and life's critical elements. You go to the movies or watch Netflix, to take a break from reality. In doing so, the world you immerse yourself in explores many elements of the human experience. You might even leave the public, or home, theatre with new insights into life, assuming the film offers such depth. Similarly, Hologram Conversations offer you a break to enter an imaginative world where you can grab some abstract popcorn and explore possibilities of your life's future, all while gaining wisdom for the present.

From these points, two potential benefits emerge from these conversations: the ability to lift one's head up from the current, all-consuming situations to gain greater perspective and the ability to take a temporary break from the oppression of the present to explore the imagination and potential of the future self.

As you come to understand the nature of Hologram Conversations, you may feel a bit intimidated. Maybe you feel that you missed the lottery with skills of imagination or creativity. You think that this practice is impossible for someone like you who cannot be so imaginative. It would feel clownish as an exercise. While it may be the case that you feel limited creatively, it may also be true that this practice remains valuable despite these obstacles. A number of ideas are presented in this book to help overcome this seeming limitation.

Even if your fears about a lack of creativity are accurate, Hologram Conversations invite a thoughtful and reflective frame of mind. This process, regardless of your personal abilities, enters a world of conversation with your future selves, which will put you on a pathway to create more opportunities for greater mindfulness and control over your inner voice.

While Hologram Conversations are only a mental exercise, and while at first blush, this exercise might seem juvenile, it is important to fully understand the process to fully ascertain its value. Once thoroughly understood and utilized, the entire Hologram Conversation is more than child's play; it can be a transformational practice that leverages your inner voice.

This chapter's general explanation of Hologram Conversations might leave the reader with more questions than answers. This is usually the case for something with utility and purpose. Complex and useful things take time to understand. At this point, it will be helpful to break down each step of the Hologram Conversation in order to elucidate the process. The next two chapters will examine the specific steps of Hologram Conversations to break down every feature further for better understanding.

Chapter 3:

Hologram Conversations Steps 1–4

We all have that inner voice that is wise, even if we don't always follow it. It's that voice I'm trying to listen to. -Ray LaMontagne

Step 1: Values First

To conduct meaningful Hologram Conversations, you will identify the most relevant content for the conversations. After all, making these conversations worthwhile might prove to be the foremost key to success. One way to examine potential content for Hologram Conversations is to ground the content upon your values or priorities in life. Values and priorities drive everything.

Topics, no matter how expedient or complex, centered on health, lifestyle choices, character traits, habits, career changes or advancements, relationships, family, and daily schedules and routines all lay upon the bedrock of your values. These are the kinds of topics ripe for enriched conversations. The key, then, is the earmark the most pertinent values and the various elements of life that arise from those values.

Not everyone feels they have figured out their values. This is fair. In fact, Hologram Conversations help identify, modify, and refine existing values. Therefore, select some values you feel could be important to you or some values you think you might vaguely follow in life. These are sufficient for a starting point. No one has to have their personal values pre-determined before engaging in Hologram Conversations.

Therefore, we begin with a survey of our personal values and priorities.

For the first step, generate a list of values and priorities. This will require a thoughtful process. Likely, you already have experience in listing, reflecting upon, or pondering your values. Now is the time to revisit your previous experiences with this and engage in your process of identifying and refining your values and priorities.

Notably, "priorities" are included with values because there are some priorities or responsibilities that cannot be ignored. You may feel that completing your taxes does not fit, explicitly, into a particular value but that it remains a necessity. As such, if you feel the need to list urgent priorities that do not fit nicely into a personal value, feel free to include these. For example, one might say that all the responsibilities that come with being a parent are a "priority," whereas "time with family" is a value. For you, these may overlap, or they are slightly exclusive items in your list of values and priorities. You might see one of these actions as a "value," with "quality time" being the value focus, while the other is seen more as a necessary set of tasks and daily chores, lovingly completed in the process of parenting. They are both inescapably critical and both part of your identity and focus as a person. The point is that both priorities and values are reasonable items to include in your list.

This value and priority-generating process itself is not the subject of this book. Feel free to use your own methods. Some people enjoy getting away to the mountains, or the beach, or to a quiet space to reflect. Some need a less extravagant and inexpensive process; they find spaces in the home, garden, workspace, public library, or park. You only need what is necessary to produce a meaningful list for yourself.

For me, I enjoy a day trek into the mountains. I meditate for a short while. I think about how my values served me in the previous year. I wonder and think back to how I lived out my values and where I could have done better. Then, I craft anywhere from five to ten values to adhere to for the year. Often, I repeat most of the values from the previous year, possibly modifying the angle or focus for that value. This becomes an annual ritual for me. For me, it is that simple; for you, it might be even more straightforward or significantly more complex. Whatever is comfortable for you, use that approach. These values, then, form the base for my Hologram Conversations, and on ideal days, order my daily life.

Values and priorities should be anything of significance to you. No doubt you have several ideas already. For those who need some inspiration, here are some possible areas to explore, randomly listed as topics, achievements, character traits, and interests:

Family	Work promotions	Running a marathon	Honesty
Love	Faith	Generosity / Helping	Hope
Relationships	Courage	Authenticity	Listening
Fishing	Bungee jumping	Balance	Speaking
Supporting others	Traveling	Providing for family	Having fun
Painting	Comfort	Safety	Strength
Laughing	Health	Entrepreneur	Dancing

Your ideas can take any form. They can be a noun or a verb.

Finally, to reiterate, bringing some sense of values is all that is needed for a Hologram Conversation. The conversation itself, over time, may help you sift through and determine your values. For now, you have a few ideas, and you will test them out in conversation with your future selves.

Once you have generated a list, save it as you will take it with you in your Hologram Conversation.

Step 2: Find an Ideal Location

The next step involves finding a distraction-free, stress-free environment for Hologram Conversations. You need a space where you can indulge in the experience fully without any obstructions. Who goes to their local cinema only to watch the film with the house lights shining bright? What cinema places windows inside the theatre, facing the busy street outside?

On the contrary, cinemas dim the lights, make windowless theatres, offer comfortable seats that might even recline, boast booming woofers, provide a wide range of drinks and food, and showcase massive screen spaces. They fully immerse you into a fantasy world with no distractions. If only every moviegoer would shut off those cell phones.

The same dedication to detail around the environment is the kind of attention you need to give to the Hologram Conversation process. You need an intentional space that facilitates the opportunity to get into a focused mental state, a zone. The windows, nearby sounds, people, furniture, time of day, level of light, and much more all need your consideration.

Even more, you want an environment that is welcoming. The space should make you feel safe and free from any outside judgment or onlookers. Because you will want the freedom to hold Hologram Conversations silently or aloud, ensuring you have privacy is important. Sometimes, you will hold the conversation in silence and peace, while at other times, you may want the experience to be more visceral, tangible, and audible. More on this later. Either way, a private and quiet space, free from distraction and welcoming, is vitally important.

On the other hand, you will want to avoid an environment so comfortable that it invites the distraction of falling asleep or mind wandering. You want to be alert and intentional throughout the process, similar to the attention necessary for meditation or yoga. For example, slouching on the couch during Hologram Conversations fails to create the kind of energy, attention, and body language conducive to a successful conversation. If this conversation you will conduct pertains to serious matters in life, as it most often will, then a balance between comfort and remaining alert is the goal to achieve. The environment should encourage this balance.

This also leads to body posture. A relaxed, neutral position helps. If you are familiar with meditative practices, sitting upright and being aware of your body and breathing are trademark components. Sitting relaxed but upright helps you release the tension in the body while maintaining a focus on the task.

As for specific locations, a dining room table can be an ideal location where you have visible chairs around the table. This can aid in the imaginary, visual "mind's eye" component of the exercise. Having that visual in front of you may ground an otherwise abstract activity into some form of concrete reality. You become more capable of picturing your future holographic selves sitting there as you turn to look at them. It adds a specific element of physicality to the imaginary aspects of a Hologram Conversation.

Really, anywhere in the home can be a haven for this process. If distraction-free, you can choose the quiet of your bedroom, the solitude and darkness of the basement, the plain space in the spare bedroom, the back porch, or the garage.

If you choose a location where you live, speak with individuals who live with you at the residence. Share with them what you are doing, in brief, so that they understand your need for a quiet and distraction-free space for a short period of time. Avoid going into the details of your process; a simple request in advance will be appreciated by all parties who live at the residence.

Additionally, this preventative notice mitigates potential awkward moments for all parties in the event that they walk in on you in the middle of a Hologram Conversation.

I find that the evenings with the lights off at the kitchen table are optimal. I speak with my family and ensure that they know what I will be doing, and we plan a time together that works for everyone. They go out of the house and have an evening out while I remain in the quiet of my home. I have also used my trips into the mountains for my Hologram Conversations. On the first day, I will meditate on, and modify, my values. The next day's focus becomes the Hologram Conversation. This wild, natural, and remote location helps me remain focused and clear of distractions.

As Hologram Conversations can occur outside the home, additional ideal locations might be your backyard, a park, or alone in nature. The enduring principle is to ensure you maintain control over distractions. Bystanders or individuals who pass by can put a halt to an otherwise successful process.

Consider additional options for an optimal location. If applicable, use your office workspace before or after people arrive. Use your car, depending on where you park. Find a vacant conference room at a hotel. Rooftops of apartment or hotel complexes can be options if not too distracting. Again, the goal is to secure a place that is quiet and free from distractions, and welcoming to facilitate a meaningful conversation.

While location selection may seem intuitive, it takes clear planning to ensure you are comfortable, alert, and free from interruptions. Hologram Conversations are a serious process, and care should be taken in finding an appropriate space.

At this point, you might have a few candidate locations in mind. Try them, and be sure to communicate your expectations and involvement in this process to any friends or family if applicable. Be flexible in case an alternative location is needed in ensuing conversations.

Step 3: Prioritize Your Mindset

The next step involves taking control of your inner voice before you initiate the Hologram Conversation. You have your values in hand, and you have an ideal location. Now, on to the practice of calming yourself.

When trying something new, combining a new experience with something familiar can be beneficial. If you have tried meditation a bit in the past or are a regular meditation practitioner, begin your Hologram Conversation with a few minutes of meditation. You will feel comfortable in an otherwise unique and novel experience. This will aid in soothing your uncertainty and help guide your concentration and openness toward the pending experience. Doing this first helps move you into the right state of mind and prepares you for the transition into a Hologram Conversation. You make critical decisions in the next few steps, so calming yourself is important for the preparation of a successful conversation.

If you are new to meditation altogether, starting with something like a short, guided meditation from an online video, application, or podcast may be helpful. It might feel intimidating to combine two new things at once, but trying something that is guided alleviates some pressure and may help you get into the right mindset for the Hologram Conversation journey you are about to begin. There are so many simple, short, guided meditations online that this step may turn out simpler than first imagined.

That said, if trying meditation is too overwhelming when simultaneously attempting Hologram Conversations for the first time, that is completely understandable. As an alternative option, simply take in a few deep breaths and then release the breath slowly over a few seconds. This alone may put you at ease and prepare you for the conversation.

Settling yourself and taking note of your state of mind prior to a Hologram Conversation makes a significant difference. The distractions of the day, the emotional burdens, and the frustrations all may hinder your success and focus. The same goes for any successes, victories, joys, and excitements; these can all act as obstacles to your focus.

For example, your morning, or day, was likely busy, full of social interactions, tasks, challenges, and delights. The thoughts from the day bounce around relentlessly in the mind; you may even rehearse events over and over without realizing it. These thoughts wear you down and drain your energy, even if positive in nature. A reset and slight distancing from all of this before jumping into a Hologram Conversation is important.

Furthermore, if you initiated the Hologram Conversation due to an important upcoming decision, experience, or challenge, then settling the mind will prove to be even more critical. You need a clear, settled mind.

You need a mind ready to explore the complexity of the topics for the conversation. If reasonable conclusions are to be reached, then this prioritizing of mindset remains paramount.

Whatever process you use, be it breathing, meditation, or some other method, make it a short, five-minute mental reset. There is no need to prolong the meditation beyond a short five-minute stint unless you really need a longer session to settle yourself.

Now, with a clear mind and a relaxed body that holds a positive posture in a quiet and distraction-free space, you can proceed to the next step.

Step 4: Identify Your Participants

With the list of values fresh in hand, a strategic location, and a settled mind, the next step is to identify and "materialize" your participants in your Hologram Conversation.

This is an opportunity to begin to see yourself with self-love and self-care. While this is an ancillary benefit, it is an important one indeed. Self-love and self-care have become topics of significance in recent decades as mental health awareness rises. As you begin to select your participants, you will be asked to see them with awe, love, respect, and honor.

A good place to begin is to identify an appropriate age near the end of your imagined life span. It should be a target age where you are still coherent and active as a person. You might estimate age eighty as your target. Maybe this version of yourself is still healthy and cogent enough to speak authoritatively into your current life. Once you have this future "self" identified, you have your first highly esteemed and respected guest invited to your Hologram Conversation.

This is your best future self near the end of life. This person you became is wise, strong, experienced, and compassionate. Not only are you seeing this precious person positively, but the feeling is mutual. Watch the tender eyes of this older person looking back at you. This older version of yourself oozes with compassion, love, and pride. Look closely, in your mind's eye, at this amazing person. This is, after all, your first honored guest at your table. Allow yourself to be in awe and feel the same awe returned toward you. Watch as the person slowly moves to a space near you, maybe a chair at the table, and gingerly sits down.

This person now sets the baseline for working backward in time toward your present self. From age eighty, you work in reverse order to discover the additional one or two guests you will ask to join you in your Hologram Conversation. Identify your future selves at different intervals of time, spread out in-between your current self and your 80-year-old self.

These next invited guests will represent a wide age range, a fully representative sample of yourself over a life span. Imagine yourself like a continuous coil representing yourself across time. Select a few links along the way in the length of that coil.

More specifically, if you are 50 years old, maybe you invite an 80-year-old version of yourself, a 70-year-old version of yourself, and a 60-year-old version of yourself.

If you are 30 years old, maybe you invite an 80-year-old version of yourself, a 60-year-old version of yourself, and a 40-year-old version of yourself.

If you are 20 years old, maybe you invite an 80-year-old version of yourself, a 55-year-old version of yourself, and a 30-year-old version of yourself.

The selection process may be arbitrary or strategic. On the more strategic side, you may elect to choose important life milestones to find candidates for your conversation. These milestones could be a year before retirement, when you become empty nesters, when you achieve financial freedom, when you plan to have children, when your children graduate, when you decide to buy that dream car, or when you plan to go on that epic vacation.

Given my age, I like to work with 10-year increments from age 85. I usually invite four total participants to my Hologram Conversation, working backward from that 85-year-old. When I first began this process, it was easier to manage only three total guests in my conversations. Now, I am comfortable talking with four different future holographic selves at my kitchen table. My attention to the process has increased and so I am able to invite an additional self into my conversations.

However, five or more, for me, seems to be too confusing and messy, with voices merging and blending incomprehensibly. Keep the conversations to a limit of three or four holographic participants.

Make sure each participant is different from each other and that each individual represents a different "season" in life. This is how you capture the many flavors of your future self. Avoid the echo chamber of three holographic selves who are on the grind and within 10 years of each other. Instead, with a range, you can achieve a variety of insights. One future holographic self might be a go-getter, career-oriented self aged in the thirties. The other may be a more reflective self, later in life, in the sixties.

Ultimately, aim for a representative sampling across time in order to seek divergent perspectives. At different stages, you will have different values and priorities. Things change; you change.

Now that you have made your final selections, you have a few future selves there in your mind's eye in front of you. Beginning to visualize them may begin to ground the abstract experience into your mind's eye. Not everyone is visually orientated, so some people may find alternative methods for grounding oneself in the Hologram Conversation process. More on this later.

~~~

My process centers on visuals to aid in my focus. I close my eyes, and I have each individual appear in my mind's eye. They appear "holographically" before me at each seat around the table. The youngest one of the three quickly shifts into the chair, full of vitality and focus. A sense of burden and burning intensity streaks across his face; he is a driven, determined future version of me. He must face challenges and explore opportunities in life. This is my 50-year-old self.

Another slowly shuffles to the chair, a gentle sigh eases off his lips, and he plops into the chair, leaving a walker wobbling to the side of him. The wrinkles of time show plainly on his face. A slight food stain rests on the right-hand side of his shirt, just below the chest. His tired, but warm, eyes slowly make their way across the table and land on me. This is my 80-year-old self.

Another walks to the chair and sits down, takes off his glasses, and rubs them clean before centering them back on the bridge of his nose. Swiveling his head around the table, he makes visual acknowledgment of the others who are present. Eventually, his eyes spot me, and he smiles. Sitting erect and with purpose, he possesses a sense of confidence with a tinge of life's accomplishments and regrets. He seems to hold a keen interest in me, not deviating from his steady gaze in my direction. This is my 65-year-old self.

I let myself drift into a bit of an imaginative state, paying attention to the wear and tear life has had on each of them. I look at the wrinkles on their hands and the coloration and knowledge in their eyes. The hair texture and colors, with their varying amounts of peppered and empty spots, manifest themselves to me. The textures of skin and clothing become clear. I perceive a few scars, physically and emotionally. The older one has a slight tremor in his left hand. The youngest of them clears his throat; some allergic agitation, I guess. The clothing each wears seems to suggest the season of life for each, depending on the need to impress.

Allowing myself this time to absorb each individual guest to my Hologram Conversation in my mind's eye, I revel and fully indulge in the moment. These are my future selves. For better or for worse, they have something to share with me, and I am honored to participate in a conversation with them.

~~~

While these representations of my future selves prove to be a bit stereotypical, they work for me. On the other hand, you may wish to imagine an energetic, nimble 80-year-old who is spontaneous, spunky, and fun, throwing all caution to the wind. You may imagine a 40-year-old who is stressed, overwhelmed, and reticent as opposed to being right in the middle of career advancement. Maybe your 60-year-old sits statuesque as someone expressing resolute determination in the face of a life crisis.

Maybe you imagine your future selves in this unique manner because you refuse to see your future selves living in some kind of unrealistic perfection or on a stereotypical trajectory, full of harmony and peace. You would rather hear from individuals who have experienced difficult times and can offer you clear advice moving forward.

The choice of the ages and the character of your Hologram Conversation guests remains entirely up to you and your imagination. In addition, it may be that for your pending topics in your Hologram Conversation, you need certain types of characters to speak wisdom to you. Simply invent the future selves you think would best impart insights.

This process of visualization, while seemingly unnecessary, is important. You must get a sense of what each future self may be thinking, feeling, and saying to you in the pending conversation. You need to know their context and current state so that you can better imagine the insights they will share. This step is especially important when you first begin Hologram Conversations, as it helps 'materialize' the otherwise immaterial in order to make an abstract process more concrete.

You have your values in hand, a helpful space, a calm mind, and your participants. With these two, three, or four individuals in front of you and fully colorized, contextualized, humanized, and texturized, and with your awareness of their character and emotional state, you may begin your Hologram Conversation.

Chapter 4:

Hologram Conversations Steps 5-8

That inner voice has both gentleness and clarity. So, to get to authenticity, you really keep going down to the bone, to the honesty, and the inevitability of something.
-Meredith Monk

Step 5: Dispositions and Beginning

The Hologram Conversation may officially begin. Your hard work setting up this process and investing in each step for success will be rewarded in due time.

Now you can prepare to speak to your holographic selves, who are sitting around you in your mind's eye. You are welcome to close your eyes at this point, keeping the images of each individual in the forefront of your mind. Closing your eyes and keeping their images in your vision can help hold your attention and avoid distraction.

While keeping your eyes closed may be your preferred approach, some may find that keeping your eyes open aids in maintaining focus. For some, keeping the eyes open helps to remain in the moment visually and to avoid allowing the mind to wander had the eyes been closed. I have found both methods, keeping the eyes open and keeping the eyes closed, work for me.

If you choose to keep your eyes open, you may enjoy interacting in small ways, smiling at each of your holographic selves to officially acknowledge their imaginary presence in front of you. This opens a whole new world where you use physicality to imagine a more concrete interaction with your future selves. The physical gestures can help merge the imaginary into the real in a more grounded sense and help you stay more committed to the process.

Whatever the choice, eyes open or closed, your disposition should be one of **curiosity** and **intrigue**. Look at these amazing future selves in front of you. A unique opportunity presents itself with great potential for gaining wisdom and insights, with some laughs and tears along the way, no doubt. Be prepared to hear their advice. They may offer rebukes, love, support, challenges, inspiration, and much more. Be ready or a range of emotional experiences with these individuals as they speak into your present life.

Even though you are the one speaking, this is a conversation. They will speak and you will listen, imaginatively, to their wisdom. As such, another disposition required for success is that of **intentional listening** and receptiveness, free from defensiveness.

You can see them there, facial expressions filled with a look of care for you. You can see their compassionate eyes. You can see their welcoming body language as they lean in to get a good look at you and offer a chuckle or two. You can feel their pride warming their faces. Or maybe they see you, and they marvel at what you are about to endure or achieve. You can discern a clear sense of hope, understanding, and compassion from them when they look at you. They seem pleased to be in this moment with you and are very thankful that you took the time to seek wisdom from them.

Imagining your future self in this way is a good opportunity to free yourself from any current self-shame shackles from life. Rather, see yourself as they would see you, with a full, endearing embrace. Any negative self-perceptions and negative self-talk will have to pause during this Hologram Conversation. You will choose to see yourself in a positive light.

Of course, you could imagine the opposite. You could embody a different disposition as you begin the conversation, one of curiosity mixed with a keen **reception toward constructive feedback**. You might, in a moment of honesty with yourself, realize you too often excuse yourself for poor habits or let things go unaddressed. Maybe you feel you genuinely need a loving kick to get yourself back on track. Your future selves could be judgmental. They could know about your recent shortcomings or what you perceive to be shortcomings, and they could be all too ready to point those out. Maybe they see some naïveté in you. Maybe you feel their biting critiques regarding your lack of experience or current state of affairs in life. If you feel this approach would be helpful, by all means, embrace it fully.

That said, something should be noted about leaning more toward your future holographic selves oozing with love toward you. The spirit of these conversations tilts more toward positivity and encouragement.

Unfortunately, most people are not allies to you. They are largely indifferent, or even worse, enemies. Even those you assume support you may not be there in challenging times when you need them. Or maybe these same people you think you can trust would change drastically for the worse if you won the lottery.

With so few people on the planet truly in your corner, supporting you through thick and thin, why not assume the positive from your future selves? At least these individuals can welcome you fully, without shame, without condescension, without hate, without loathing, without manipulation, and without conditional approval. No, you have permission to invite the most allied, caring future selves to your Hologram Conversation. They want what is best for you, even if that means some tough love statements and some best-intentions judgments. Regardless of their input, you may imagine them to have unequivocally the absolute, unadulterated best in mind for you.

To be honest, we even struggle to be allied to ourselves. Self-dislike and scorn remain common among even the best of us. It is exceedingly difficult to love yourself. Even if you find it challenging to care for yourself, even if self-love is a struggle to maintain, at least the Hologram Conversations can be an oasis. This imaginative exercise can unite you with future holographic versions of yourself that embody an enthusiastic, pastoral tone. Seeing your future selves in this light will only serve to guide you toward a more open and honest Hologram Conversation with your future selves. The choice is yours, but I recommend you lean toward the unabashedly supportive future selves.

If we were to zoom out a bit from the Hologram Conversation itself and see this process from a more clinical perspective, we can recognize that this is a creative process that helps you see yourself in a more positive light. Moreover, you see yourself in a positive light over time. This is a profound mental exercise, regardless of the strict adherence to the steps in the Hologram Conversation. As ridiculous and inauthentic as things may feel in these initial moments of sharing, this mindful practice is helpful even if you are not "feeling the creative flow" or "properly imagining your future selves." Once the awkwardness subsides, you can feel the effects of positive self-talk that works toward constructing a better present self.

Once the conversation begins, it is not about getting it right or following a perfect formula of speech. This is not about doing it perfectly the first time, or any time for that matter. Hologram Conversations, done well, take time to mold and customize to your own liking and benefit.

Be patient with yourself. Give yourself permission to chuckle at the apparent silliness of the entire thing at first. Yes, admit it, you are talking to imaginary selves. This is okay. It is entirely in the imagination. Your feelings are completely understandable. Notice them and then proceed to the next step in the conversation.

Indulge fully in the process, and you will see what this "fake" and "imaginative" conversation can elicit. Authentic self-examination and reflection are what will emerge, and they will leverage your inner voice for the purposes of personal growth and decision-making navigation.

You now have all participants in your mind's eye, and you are clear about your dispositions.

Step 6: Speaking

With the participants clearly before you and your intention to engage established, you may begin speaking to them. Whether silently internal or aloud, it does feel a little interesting at first. It may be helpful to remind yourself that this whole process is simply the self-talk referred to in chapter one. This inner voice already runs in the background. You are hijacking it and making it work for you for a brief time. Simply, you are utilizing this natural, inner practice in a more purposeful way. Once you get into the imaginary conversation and words begin to flow, it feels more comfortable and natural. It does take some practice before you feel fully comfortable with having a conversation when, in reality, no one is physically there in front of you.

The first order of business is to discuss your values with your future selves. You have the list in mind or physically in front of you. Share your current values and priorities in full detail with your holographic selves and why you hold these values or priorities. List each one and defend them honestly. Explain why they are valuable to you at this time. Give examples of why they are important. Share how these values impact your life in one way or another.

Details are critical at this stage. Get it all out there on the "table," open and honest. No one is there to judge you; this is your chance to put "airtime" to your values and hear them spoken aloud, literally, or in your head silently. Make sure everything that matters to you is clearly articulated to your holographic selves for them to consider. The whole time, they will be listening without any input. Watch their facial expressions in your mind's eye and find joy in sharing your genuine self in this moment with your future selves.

If we are to zoom out again and see this from an objective point of view, what you are doing, in fact, is vocalizing your values and priorities out loud or silently in your mind. This process, of course, helps expose them out in the open. When you share your ideas out loud, the brilliance and foolishness of them become all too clear. When we make our ideas verbal, they are then made available for scrutiny and refining. This is exactly what we are aiming for in this loving, calm, and caring environment in the Hologram Conversation. It is a mixture of transparency, self-care, and growth.

While you are vulnerable in this moment, it is important not to judge anything at this time. Let what you shared be there for your future selves to examine. Do not apologize or retract anything. Simply share openly with them.

This part of the conversation is rich and beautiful. What typically happens for most of us is that our values go unidentified or possibly ignored. They exist but deep down under the piles and piles of life's daily endeavors. We have a propensity to find ourselves lost in the minutiae of life, forgetting a deeper purpose or meaning. Hell, we might be too exhausted from our work to even bother.

Even worse, if our values emerge in reflection or discussion with others, we imagine self-defeaters that mock those values. We abuse our own values, imagining that we do not deserve them or that we just fail to have the time or effort needed to care. With your future selves about to chime in on your ideas, you will be able to hear compassionate, empathic responses to your values and priorities.

For some of us, this is the first time anyone has ever truly heard our values, affirmed them, and helped us work through them. Cherish this opportunity to discard the all too easy dismissal of your values and to embrace what insights your future selves will eventually share about your values and priorities.

On the other hand, some of us are very good at articulating our values and priorities. We practice positive self-talk, and we embrace our own values. We move beyond mere goal orientation to really seek the deeper values we hold. We possess the time and opportunity for this; we are so privileged.

Maybe we are situated in amazing families who love us and show compassion and empathy regularly, affirming our priorities and values. If you are blessed in this way, then this stage in the Hologram Conversation is yet another affirmation of your direction in life and who you are as a person. It acts as another celebration, another confirmation that you are walking the path you want.

Now that you have shared your values, the next step is to share your **life's work**. You might be wondering, at this point, if this is a monologue or a conversation. The conversation is coming soon. You simply need some time to share your ideas aloud without any interruptions before your future selves weigh in on anything. There will be several areas of life that you will share, without interruption, with your future selves for them to examine and consider for the back and forth that comes later.

You can now share about your daily life. If applicable, it may include any of the following: career work, responsibilities, friends, family experiences and needs, enemies, upcoming opportunities, chores, hobbies, and to-do lists. Lay it all bare in front of them. Let this be a self-audit of sorts, just without any judgment.

What consumes your time? What consumes your energy? What consumes your thinking? Share all the busy aspects of life for your future selves to consider. In essence, the conversation, to this point, has been a summary of your life's being and work, beginning with values and now listing the daily, monthly, and yearly realities.

After sharing your values and then daily life, the next area to share openly is about your **relationships**. These relationships are the kind that fit into categories such as romantic, work / career-related, and platonic. Which relationships are growing? Which ones are suffering? Which relationships do you wish you had? Which ones do you need to develop? Which ones do you need to set boundaries? Which relationships encourage you and build you up? Which ones bring you down?

Share everything openly so that your future selves may listen and consider everything you say. Do not be afraid to go into detail. This may be the most vulnerable part of the Hologram Conversation. This is a private time, though. Remember, it is ultimately with you and you alone, so there is great liberation to speak and let it out. Avoid hesitation and share, even if they include dark fears or fantastical impossibilities. Lay it all out to bear. Your future selves are looking at you with sheer delight and genuine empathy. Pleasure overwhelms them as they hear all the juicy details, good, bad, and ugly. You hold their unabandoned support and their unabashed gazes. Be confident and rest at ease when you share.

Now, you can pivot from sharing about general relationships to familial-focused relationships. The same questions can be explored but in direct relation to immediate and extended family members. Here are some family units, if applicable, to consider, not in any particular order. What about your spouse? Your children? Your mother? Your father? Your siblings? Guardians? Foster family? Adopted family? Grandparents? Extend out as far as your currently active relationships extend.

What is the health of these relationships? Which ones are struggling? Which ones are beautiful and healing and uplifting? Again, put everything out there in the open for vulnerable examination. You may be entering an even more vulnerable stage in the Hologram Conversation at this point. Stay fixed, in your mind's eye, on the empathy and the warmth seen in their eyes. They have your best in mind.

Bear in mind that there is no perfect family. There can be unforgettably beautiful moments and the most vile, forgettable moments in families. The whole range of possibilities can be shared with your future selves.

Something to consider in advance of sharing about family, and friends for that matter, is the potential to trigger deep pain and hurt. Please proceed with caution in these stages of the conversation. If you have experienced abuse or deep pain in your relationships, it may be appropriate to avoid these parts of the Hologram Conversation, saving those explorations for opportunities in the presence of a mental health professional. It is your personal judgment regarding the appropriateness of the inclusion of relationships in your Hologram Conversations. The expressed purpose, if you do wish to include potentially triggering relationship histories in your Hologram Conversation, would be for self-healing alone. There should be no self-harm that results from a Hologram Conversation. Protect yourself; you know what you can and cannot handle safely.

You may extend beyond the current family and friends to share a bit about the family and friend relationships that you miss. Whatever the cause of the loss, it may be particularly healing to revisit how you miss them and what those relationships meant to you during your Hologram Conversation. Allow yourself that time to reminisce and mourn and smile in their memories. Again, a note about anything triggering applies. If necessary, skip this portion of the sharing.

At this point, you have discussed values, current life activities, relationships, family, and any relationships you may have lost over time. Again, pay close attention to how your holographic selves watch you. Look at their caring tones. Allow any relevant emotions to emerge. Allow yourself to feel, even if imaginary, the embrace of your future selves toward you. They also miss the ones you miss. They also feel the same joys and pains in your relationships as you do. They were you; they understand. They remember when they had your current values and priorities. They remember the hustle and grind of your daily activities.

They understand you and love you. **Feel this moment fully before proceeding**.

The next area of life to share with your holographic selves is the **obstacles** that you face. This is going to be a shift from a highly emotional stage of relationship sharing to a slightly more objective, emotion-free sharing. In contrast to the previous sharing, where you lingered in the space for a while, allowing emotions to materialize, this is not a sharing point where you pause and dwell. On the contrary, this is a swift stage in the process.

Begin sharing about obstacles. Who is standing in your way? What is standing in your way? Is it someone at work? Someone in the family? Maybe it is your own perceived self-inadequacies? Is it a lack of money? Is it where you live? Your health?

List and describe each obstacle. Avoid devolving to complaining, feeling sorry for yourself, or getting into a negative head space. Speak each obstacle calmly and objectively, with personal distance. Observe them and name them and then leave them there on the "table" for your Holographic selves to consider.

This is not a time to go on bitter diatribes about who has wronged you. If you have lived any amount of time in life, then you have wronged people, and people have wronged you. This is life's reality. Things have been unfair; pretty much everyone on this planet experiences unfair realities, and we all end up six feet under in the end, even the most privileged among us. What is important in this stage is to avoid snagging in this stage of the Hologram Conversation. Allow this stage to be your honest acknowledgment of the genuine obstacles you face.

After honestly exploring your current obstacles, you have one final thing to share with your holographic selves. Offer a quick two to three-sentence snapshot of you as a whole and how you are holding up in the midst of everything life is throwing at you.

How are you doing, really? Share this candidly and openly. Your future selves need to hear this. You need to hear your own self share this. You might say something like, "To sum it all up, while I value family, work has really gotten in the way lately. Thankfully, I have that handful of friends I told you about who hold me up right now and really support me. It's difficult. I want more time with family, and I need to be more financially secure to do this. I need some wisdom. Thank you all for listening."

Something simple and honest like this is the aim at the end of this stage of the Hologram Conversation.

During this initial sharing time in its totality, you have essentially laid your entire self bare for your holographic selves to see, hear, and honor. How blessed are you to share this with your future selves, and how blessed are they to hear this from you? While imaginative, of course, there is no other situation in life that allows such an opportunity.

It should be said at this point that we know what is really happening behind the scenes of a Hologram Conversation. This is a trick of conducting a self-analysis and self-inventory. It is a creative method of doing something we all know how to do in one form or another in a fresh and positive manner. With a specific process such as a Hologram Conversation, we can indulge in this practice of self-analysis and self-inventory more often and with self-love as the foundation.

At this stage of the Hologram Conversation, it has only been a self-audit. It sets the stage for the magic that comes later when the back and forth commences. Even so, this stage of openly examining one's life is beneficial regardless of the next steps of Hologram Conversations.

The next step is where the process begins to look like a conversation. Some people might suggest that the speaking part should be broken into smaller segments, with the opportunity for the future selves to share back and forth sooner in the conversation. It would look more like one item at a time shared, values and priorities first, and then a back-and-forth discussion that follows.

While there is truth to this idea, it is more important that you share unimpeded in the first part of a Hologram Conversation. Airing it all without any setbacks or disruptions is key. If you stop at each stage of sharing, you may find yourself derailed at some point, only to never reach the end of your talking points. Furthermore, you may become quite frustrated at some point with what you imagine your future selves are sharing. This could stunt the success of the Hologram Conversation. You are better served to run through each talking point before you ever "hear" a response from your future holographic selves.

Sharing continuously, almost as in a stream-of-consciousness approach, without judgment or feedback from your imaginary future selves, helps to release all the tension and put everything out in the open. If you happen to forget some things in the back and forth later, it is okay. The aim is not to solve and examine everything in your life in one Hologram Conversation. Instead, you have a menu from which you can select and choose what parts of your life will be discussed. If you miss anything, you can discuss it in the next Hologram Conversation you host.

At this stage in the process, you have made these values a priority just by the very nature of reflecting upon them thus far in the conversation. You have given airtime to these important aspects of your life. You have begun to weigh through each topic. By verbalizing these things, you have thought more clearly about them.

Step 7: Listening

After having shared so much so quickly, you might feel a bit tired, emotionally and physiologically. Take a few moments in silence and breathe. Let your mind rest on the words you just shared and relax. As with the outset of this Hologram Conversation, a few minutes of meditation may help to center you before the next step begins. You may also remain silent, focusing on a single positive word to regain your energy for the next step.

These few moments may feel awkward in the silence with no activity at all. Maybe you feel vulnerable. Maybe everything feels anticlimactic after all that hard work expressing everything inside you. Maybe you still see the holographic selves staring at you, and it makes you uncomfortable. Maybe you are wondering why you ever tried such a cockamamie thing in the first place.

On the other hand, maybe you feel energized and ready. You anticipate interesting ideas from your future selves as they discuss the things you have shared. Maybe you even feel a bit anxious, anticipating their thoughts.

If you are experiencing these thoughts and feelings, they are a normal reaction to something new and unusual. How you proceed to the next step makes all the difference.

After spending a few moments in silence to rest and meditate, you may calmly and gently emerge from that step to the listening step of the Hologram Conversation. This is the intentionally silent part of the practice. As with any step in this process, you may do this with your eyes opened or closed. I enjoy doing this step with my eyes open.

As you sit in silence, your imagination now takes control. Your mind's eye will animate the future selves who are sitting around you. Begin to hear each participant engage and speak. Listen carefully to what each holographic self says. You might find that they all begin to emerge with something to say and begin interrupting each other as they speak to you.

You can imagine the initial chaos. If their imaginary words in your mind become overwhelming and jumbled because everyone is speaking over each other, then speak to them and give permission to only one individual to speak at a time. As it is entirely in your own mind, you choose who speaks and in what order. This process of intentionally, in silence or aloud, requesting one speaker at a time will help you narrow the focus in your mind's eye.

As each person speaks, listen without judgment. Seek their insight. This opportunity to hear from your future selves is what makes this process unique. You will hear each of them begin to react to what you shared in step six of the Hologram Conversation. This is not a back-and-forth just yet.

This is only them speaking to you, encouraging you, lifting you up, and wondering about things you shared. They might be reacting to your values, your busy schedule, your obstacles, or your relationships. One might react to one topic while another holographic self reacts to another topic. If you listen carefully and with patience, they will speak, and their wisdom will emerge.

Now that they are speaking one at a time, and things seem to be moving along, take a deep breath. Stay attentive and listen to what they say. I repeat this command because it is too easy to derail this process by losing the train of thought or allowing the mind to wander. It takes discipline to ensure you remain in a conversation that is abstract and within the mind only.

As they speak, take note of what they acknowledge. Who is speaking? How is this person sharing with compassion toward you? Are your obstacles being affirmed? Are your successes being affirmed? Does each future self want to hold you and let you know everything will be okay? Does one have a cautious frown? How about an inquisitive smile? Read their body language and facial expressions as they speak. Look for the beauty in each of them and take in their wisdom.

Zooming out again, this illustrates just how powerful the human mind is when given a particular task. Really, the wisdom and insights observed emerge from your current self. It is merely the framework that pulls them to the surface. This is a self-explorative process where you seek to understand yourself better, and each new step in the conversation may be particularly revelatory and potentially shocking.

As noted before, if the visual elements are too challenging to imagine, then focus on their words alone. The visual elements will come with practice and experience.

Listen for a while. I am certain they have plenty to say about what you shared. You were transparent with everything. Now, they need a chance to be transparent in return with you. Be careful not to wander at this point. The reality of the situation is that the room is silent, and you are listening to what really amounts to your own inner thoughts. Find a method to remain engaged—a physical movement, more visualization, and verbal acknowledgments such as "oh," "ok," and "interesting" might keep you rooted in the moment.

Some individuals may want to take notes as they listen. I like to listen exclusively. However, there is merit to taking notes as you hear ideas coming from your holographic selves. This is especially true is multiple, new ideas emerge. You will want to capture it. Just ensure that the process of writing does not distract you from this critical time of listening or put an end to the continuous flow of their conversation.

At this point, what was once individuals speaking to you might evolve into a dialogue among themselves. What might be observed is the beginning of a rich conversation among your future selves while you remain silent, listening, and watching. They may even begin to interact with each other quite passionately.

This is where the pearls of wisdom begin to be found in the Hologram Conversation. Even though everything comes only from your own mind, framing your inner voice in this way reveals the most incredible insights.

You can expect intriguing interactions. In fact, you can expect to observe strident disagreements at times. I find this to be the most fascinating part of the entire process. You will discover that your future selves have conflicting interests and values at different ages.

They may disagree with things you have said. One might share an idea, and another might add to it or even challenge it. They may begin offering you advice or the next steps you should take. Maybe their advice is conflicting. All of this is normal. Simply listen and absorb everything.

One speaks up and makes a recommendation, only to see another argue about something different. Even though they disagree, the present "you" will glean their thoughts and make conclusions at the end of the process, so you do not need to intervene in your future selves' disagreements. Those disagreements are there for a reason. Both perspectives have something valuable to offer.

Remember, they come from different stages of life with different experiences and motivations. Avoid ostracizing one of the participants on age alone. Just because the elderly holographic self has lived longer does not mean that person has a monopoly on truth. Maybe that elder self is jaded and exhausted, offering flippant advice out of a place of hurt. Maybe your younger selves are clearer-headed and have wiser directions for you at your current phase of life. Maybe in order to arrive at the elder's satisfied state, the advice from the younger versions of yourself proves invaluable. Be open to any possibility. They all, each of your future holographic selves, have something to offer you.

Each person speaking offers a window of insight for you, and a way to gain perspective on your current values, endeavors, and relationships, and how they may shift over time.

After listening for some time, you can begin to make sense of what they are saying to you. What are their overall feelings toward you and your current state of affairs in life? What specific elements of your life are they proud of, and which ones do they recommend you course correct? What themes are emerging?

What should be made of the content of their ideas? Are they asking you to think more about certain values over other values? Maybe they recommend you say "no" to a project and spend more time with a loved one. They could challenge one or more of your values, questioning your commitment to that value or priority. They might remind you of something you need to address at this time of life. Possibly, they offer a warning.

Maybe they offer you inspiration and encouragement. You might hear one suggest trying a new hobby even though you are worried about the time commitment, or you are nervous to start altogether. Suddenly, another has an idea for pushing your career forward. Is it possible they note some ways to overcome obstacles?

On the contrary, maybe verbose, passionate, and constant chatter is not what you observe. They could simply sit in silence and think, catalyzing your own thinking within the silence. Maybe the pace of the conversation is slow, with insights and suggestions coming every so often with several minutes of silence in between. All of these outcomes are wonderful.

Typically, my Hologram Conversations prove lively and active. As these conversations are an extension of you and your mind, the nature of these conversations themselves may reveal something about your personality. It seems impossible that everyone's Hologram Conversation will look and sound the same. These conversations should act like a unique fingerprint. No two conversations among people should be the same. They are fully personalized and run by you in your own mind. You are the driver.

Maybe for you, the conversations are more hushed and thoughtful. For someone else, they might be particularly strong, even contentious at times. Yet, for others, their conversations are bright and enthusiastic. Still, others might manifest as especially warm. Who knows how your conversations look and feel until you engage fully.

In all, give your future selves at least ten minutes to speak during this step. Sometimes I get lost in their words and spend much longer; this is appropriate so long as you remain engaged in the process. Their conversation can last up to an hour if you let it. The duration of their sharing is entirely up to you and your enjoyment of the exercise. Time is not the point. What is learned and understood are the points.

Also, notice that there is a sort of meditation that is occurring simultaneously with the exercise. Although your mind is quite active throughout, the signature element is that the mind remains focused on a singular idea or train of thought the entire time, free from distraction from outward stimuli. The ability to focus on one thing over time results in the mind muscle being developed in this step. This entire step in the conversation becomes a sort of pseudo-meditative, self-reflective, perspective-taking, perspective-sharing, self-challenging, and self-affirming experience, all wrapped into one moment in time.

Step 8: Dialogue

Now that you have been silent for some time, anywhere from ten minutes to an hour, you may begin a dialogue with your holographic selves. This is the back-and-forth you have been waiting for all along. At this point, it can finally be labeled a conversation. Structure begins to fade away during this step. It is a free-for-all conversation. With the groundwork completed, a free-flowing conversation can be held with grace, wisdom, knowledge, context, patience, and purpose.

Before a breakdown of a potential dialogue, a review of each step might be helpful, especially in more objective terms.

Objectively, what you have done is share your life's important aspects in an empty space, and then you sat in silence for a period of time. When you shared, it was either audible or silent in your mind. In reality, you have articulated and verbalized your values and priorities, your relationships, your work, and your obstacles. You have brought them to the surface and expressed them in words. Furthermore, you engaged in a thought experiment whereby you listened to imagined future versions of yourself deliberate on everything you openly shared with them. You meditated on these imaginary words and pondered how they might inform your current practices in life.

In the abstract, you began a conversation, unbelievably, with different future versions of yourself. The ideas shared were inspiring and shocking at times. You were fascinated by them, and they were, in turn, fascinated with you. The honor and respect pervaded over the conversation, and you indulged in something odd but beautiful. While difficult to put a finger on it, you might almost say this was a sort of spiritual experience and mental healing. Clarity around your current state in life was birthed, and you felt support from your future selves throughout.

$$\sim\sim\sim$$

Now, you may begin an open-ended dialogue. I enjoy doing this out loud and listening to answers in silence. As per any previous step in the Hologram Conversation, you may engage in silence and allow the dialogue to be solely within the mind, or you may make the process audible, speaking on your current self's perspectives in response to your future self's ideas.

Begin by responding to the ideas shared from step seven of the Hologram Conversation. Pick the most important item to you and speak to them. Agree with them. Debate them. Challenge them. Thank them. Combine their ideas with yours. Nuance their ideas by accepting some parts and discarding others. Add clarification from your own perspective. Ask for clarification from them. Ask for elaboration on a particular point. Stay curious.

After you speak your mind, listen again to what they have to say. Try to remain open, teachable, vulnerable, and curious as they respond. Let the back and forth transpire while avoiding defensiveness. Engage meaningfully, seeking to understand more than seeking to be understood. The whole purpose is to hear from them as opposed to you convincing them of anything. Always avoid this form of self-deception.

As the back-and-forth, agreeing and disagreeing, sharing, and supporting occurs, there are no set steps, stages, or formulas. This is completely personalized, and the conversation will be in the direction you take it.

Remember that this is now an open-ended dialogue. You are allowed to interrupt them, and they will interrupt you. It should be an energized discussion among your holographic selves and you in your chosen space.

As rounds of conversations continue, test them and then listen to their responses. Pose thoughtful questions that dig deeper. Do not accept anything less than a thoroughly explored session. If you have invested this much time already, then tap into the true power of this process by settling for nothing less than true clarity and direction in your life. Continue critiquing, questioning, clarifying, and accepting. Most importantly, continue listening.

After concluding in one area of life, you can move on to the next idea of importance to you. Accordingly, the entire iterative process recycles. The back-and-forth, the challenges and questioning, and the clarifying all cycle through once again, only this time regarding the new area of life you wish to explore.

Continue cycling through topics until you are satisfied or too tired to continue. If taken seriously, this process is exhausting but beautifully exhausting. The only work worth doing is the kind that is meaningful and difficult. Most likely, this Hologram Conversation facilitates a personal life dig at a depth explored infrequently, if ever. It takes work to genuinely explore these areas of life to this level and to stay focused on the task.

Overall, I find this final step of the Hologram Conversation to be the most substantive of the entire process. You may find yourself arguing or even negotiating with future versions of yourself. This can be a lively conversation, to say the least. It all depends on how you and your participants engage in the process. It can also be, once you have practiced and built up stamina, the longest step in the process.

You might even have to engage in conflict resolution at times. You and one of your future selves may need to find consensus even though you disagree on an issue. For example, if you have a side hustle you love, but one of your future selves suggests it is harmful to your health and intrusive upon your time, you need to negotiate with that future self until you find common ground. It could be that you limit the side hustle. Or maybe you remove it altogether. Sometimes, consensus is not possible, and you have to ignore the advice of your future self and proceed with the status quo.

In this example, it could also be that one of your future selves approves of the side hustle but with some minor modifications, whereas an older future self says to remove it completely. Now, the three of you must discuss and negotiate until you come to clarity on what you will do with this side hustle in your life. When there are three of you negotiating together, you almost forget that this is an imaginative process that is wholly within your own mind. You can get blissfully lost, in a positive way, in the conversation that you might forget that you are the only one in the space speaking. It is a beautiful thing when this happens to me. In these moments, I suddenly realize I have tapped into the potential of these conversations.

After reading the breakdown of a Hologram Conversation, you may be unclear about the specifics of the conversation and how it plays out. The next chapter will provide a sample Hologram Conversation to provide further clarity.

Chapter 5:

Sample Hologram Conversation

Your inner voice is the voice of divinity. To hear it, we need to be in solitude, even in crowded places. -A. R. Rahman

This chapter contains a sample Hologram Conversation. In other words, if a Hologram were to be recorded and put into a script, the following is how it might read. This sample presents a simplistic and generic sample from steps six through eight in Chapter 4.

Prior to reading the following sample, the reader must understand that a generic example will feel devoid of authentic details. It will read slightly sterile and predictable because everything is fictitious and intended to resonate with a wide range of readers. The sample may feel contrived as it is not aligned with a real person's values, relationships, responsibilities, and obstacles.

Simply, it is a hypothetical conversation with a hypothetical person and that person's hypothetical future selves. That said, there should be items that feel genuine to you. The breadth of the sample affords the opportunity for connection on some level.

The only way the Hologram Conversation process becomes genuine is if you undergo the process with commitment. The sample model in this chapter will highlight a basic sense of Hologram Conversations, but it will also highlight the critical need for a highly engaged participant for authenticity to be discovered in this process.

In the following model you will come to know the basic parameters of the conversation and understand steps six through eight in greater detail. You will gain a functional understanding.

Sample Hologram Conversation (Steps 6-8)

We begin at step six. In this sample, hypothetically, steps one through five were completed already. Values were noted through a strategic and personal process, a location conducive to the conversations was secured, meditation was used to help the participant find the right frame of mind, three holographic future selves were identified and imagined in full detail, and a full embrace of the context and the personalities of each holographic self became clear to the participant. The participant is fully ready to engage in the holographic conversation.

Additionally, given the purpose of this chapter, it will be longer than the other chapters as it encapsulates an entire Hologram Conversation.

The conversation below is written in an informal, congenial tone to set the standard for a typical Hologram Conversation. The conversation attempts to represent someone fairly new to Hologram Conversations with some hesitations, uncertainties, and insecurities. This representation is to align more closely with the readers who will soon undergo the process and potentially feel similarly reticent at first.

The voice, characterization, and tone of the imaginary speaker may not resonate with you nor sound like a compelling character. Keep in mind that the purpose of this chapter is not to craft a wondrous fictional world fit for a novel but rather to communicate a basic sample to the reader.

As a final note, there will be places in the script below where there are intentional brackets and a comment inside saying to "insert" something such as a name, medical condition, or restaurant. This is intentional to allow the reader to import a bit of their own contexts along the way. The more specificity provided, the more this "general" sample collapses.

Step 6 [Speaking]

[participants include a character "You," whose given name is River. River is the person engaging in the Hologram Conversation, and the holographic selves are a 40-year-old River, a 60-year-old River, and an 80-year-old River]

You: Well, guys, here we are, all of us. Good evening. As usual, this is a bit interesting imagining you all here. As you know, in the next few minutes, I want to share some things about where I'm at right now in life in a general sense. I'll be talking about some of the values I think I have right now. Also, I'll be talking about some of my priorities and responsibilities. Adding to those areas, I will share with you all about the relationships I have going right now, both with my family and outside of my family. I think I'll have time to discuss some challenges I'm facing as well. So, yeah, that's about it.

[pause]

Beginning with my values. Alright, where to start? Well, I've been wondering if I even think about my values enough to be honest. I like to think I have them, and I know I do. But I don't usually think about them as often or as deeply as I did getting ready for this conversation. In preparation for this conversation, I had some time to reflect, and I have values I want to run by you all and see what you think.

["You" pulls out a paper with values written on it]

First off, I'll just list them, and then I'll explain each one and what I think they mean to me, at least at this time. Subject to change, I'm sure. So, yeah, I would say that I value relationships, getting a decent amount of exercise, and my career, I guess. I mean, it matters to me, but it gets old; my one hobby, the only one I really have time for these days [chuckle]. You know how it is—that daily grind.

Ultimately, in a perfect world, these are, I don't know […], some of my values. I'm not sure how often I follow them, though. Maybe that's something we can talk about, you know, making these more of a priority somehow [pause]. Well, that's the list anyway. I'd like to sort of break them down now and share why I think these are my values.

As for relationships, I guess I'm pretty happy with what I have going on right now. I mean, I think relationships are important, of course. I've had some good relationships in the past and some not-so-good ones, as you all know [chuckle]. I guess I find that having friends is sort of an important part of being healthy, but I don't really go about it intentionally. I just, I don't know, have some friends. Anyway, when I think about people who are sort of unhealthy emotionally or psychologically, I kind of think about people who are a bit withdrawn and disconnected from others. You just need people around you.

I mean, it's a double-edged sword in a way. People can and will hurt you, and people can lift you up, too. So, I would say I value relationships right now, but I guess recent experiences in life are teaching me to be a bit cautious and more guarded at the same time. Not sure if that's a good thing or not. Maybe I'm just getting grumpy and old [sigh].

So, I'm happy where I'm at. I'm just not sure if I'm on the right track, though, and finding a good balance.

[few seconds pause]

Ok, for exercise, I value exercise because it's important to me. I mean, it sounds a bit funny and cliché, I admit it. But it is. My grandfather passed away at a young age, and I'm willing to bet that had he been in better shape, he wouldn't have suffered like he did. The same goes for my dad, too. More exercise would have really helped him reduce some of his current health issues and prolonged his life. I guess I kind of look at it and think that it's something maybe I can control a bit.

So, for me, I just want to live reasonably long and healthy. I want to be there for my daughter in the future. Looks like each of you kept up some exercise. You all look like you're in good shape. Good job, all of you [chuckle].

[few seconds pause]

Next, for my career, it's important because I know that I need to provide for my daughter. My partner works too so that helps a lot. I guess it's just important to keep up my work and really make sure I contribute to creating a stable home of sorts. I don't like how much I have to work, you know, but I have to make it work because of our financial needs.

[few seconds pause]

Okay, as for hobbies, I value them because I think they round out a person. It can't always be about work and stuff. I used to have so many side interests in the past. I was younger and had more time. I probably should have invested more at that age and gotten more serious about my career, but I'm happy that I played around a bit. Anyway, those younger days were filled, as you know, with poker nights, bowling, some hiking here and there, road trips with friends, and jamming to some music with the band. I guess most of these childhood interests have faded a bit over time, but I still value them, I think.

I suppose you can sort of grow out of them in a way. I do have one right now that I play around with a little--the guitar. I mean, it makes me happy. I enjoy playing. I just don't have as much time to enjoy it as I would like. But it brings back those younger days. I feel alive even in my sloppy playing.

[few seconds pause]

That's about it for my values right now. There are other things that I think are important, but for today's conversation, I just wanted to throw these few values and priorities out there to discuss with each of you. Maybe you can tell me I'm off my rocker or something. Or maybe you can assure me I'm doing what I need to do.

[few seconds pause]

Before we talk about my values, I do have a few more things to share. I want to take a few minutes to tell you about what's consuming a lot of my time right now so that you get a better picture of everything— basically, just the busy parts of life.

As for my work, it's the usual. The day-to-day is real, you know what I mean? My co-workers are, well, you know; let's just say there are good days and there are crap days with more bad ones than good ones. [sigh] Drama, you know? Well, anyway, despite what they told us in school growing up, work isn't supposed to be some life's call. I'll make it, don't worry. Other people have it worse off than me. You all made it to the points you're at, so I'm sure I'm on the right path. Just need to keep up with all the work. It's so draining. I feel like I sometimes come home a shell of myself and unable to, like, be there, if you know what I mean.

Even in the social turmoil at work, at least you'd hope for a chance to move up. I don't see much room for upward movement in the company. Maybe there's something, but I don't see it. It's frustrating. But I have a couple of friends who are suffering without jobs right now. So, I guess you must find the positive side even in less ideal times and situations. So, in a way, work is fine. It consumes me, but I get a paycheck. Uncle Sam takes most of it and I eke out a living on the rest.

Beyond the job, it's all about getting home and doing whatever needs to be done around the house. You guys all know what I'm talking about; it's the usual. The constant list of things to fix or figure out. The trips into town. The bills. You'd think things would run themselves more easily these days with all this technology around us. Anyway, that stuff usually sucks up a bunch of evenings for me. And what's really frustrating is things aren't resolved as fast as I'd expect, either. Whatever I'm working on, gets pushed to tomorrow for one reason or another. And on and on it goes.

After whatever things need to be done around the house, the remaining time is divvied up among dinner, some time on my phone, and then bed. Crazy. It's not all bad. I don't want to paint a picture of a life buried in misery or something like that. I'm not suffering, really. But it's definitely not the promise of the dream life that you dreamt about as a child. Adult is a pain in the […] you know what.

Weekends are a mixed bag at times with me and my partner, so that's a bit more unpredictable. Sometimes, we're doing things around the house and errands and stuff, and other times we just chill and watch shows all day. Weekends, sometimes, are that release valve from the pressure of the week.

Basically, I feel exhausted by the time I crawl to Friday.

[few seconds pause]

[sigh] I do have that hobby that I dabble with from time to time, like I said. I like playing the guitar, as you all know. It's something I've always wanted to develop further. I was good, and then walked away from it and lost some of those skills. Thankfully, I do find some time to take it out and pluck away every so often. I wish I was a bit more serious about it, but it is what it is. I mean, it would be nice to really get into it a bit more.

My daughter joins me sometimes when I play. She sings along with songs that she knows. When she shows up on the couch next to me, I start thinking back to the songs that I knew as a kid. It makes me happy to play songs from my younger years for some reason, and it makes me happy to see her happy. She's a trip, though. She's a complete gem, guys. I really cherish these moments I get with her.

Anyway, hopefully, I can take up some more hobbies in the future or get more serious about this one. Who knows, we'll see.

[few seconds pause]

I'd like to share a bit about my relationships now if that's okay.

I'll start with some of my general friendships. I've got a couple of friends from work, [insert name here] and [insert name here]. They're good people. We talk. We do some things together. And we usually get together around sporting events, and sometimes we meet at our local pub on 3rd Street. I really enjoy them, but our relationships aren't that deep. They're just work friends, you know. It's the whole hang out and gossip about work after work kind of thing.

I do have a good friend from high school. We meet up every few months or so. We meet at the driving range in town, where we grab our irons and smack a few around, and grab a few drinks. I find that I can be open with [insert name here]. I like how [insert name here] speaks from the heart and just tells it like it is. We share some good memories too and those times we reminisce are good.

My partner and I also have a few shared friends. We go to some concerts at times, and we've done the casual hiking thing a few times in the past. We usually do something together a few times a year. We visited Aruba once. That was cool. We've hit up Vegas a couple of times. It was fun. They're good friends.

Other than that, I hang out at [insert restaurant name] sometimes with [insert name] and [insert name]. We grab a bite and just talk about nothing. We get together a few times a year or so. We mostly play it by ear. It's a thing, a time to just hang, not much more.

I feel like I have some solid friends, but when I list them out, it seems like so few at the same time. Maybe I need to get out there a bit more. I mean, I'm happy with my friends. I wonder, though, if they lift me up enough. Anyway, we'll talk about this later in the conversation, I'm sure.

[few seconds pause]

I'd like to talk about the closer relationships, too. Mainly my family. I'd start with my partner. For now, I'd say that [insert name here] is a wonderful, intimate friend. Things are going well. We had a bit of a fight recently, though. It was about how we spend time on weekends. We're both pretty tired from work, and we have some different ideas about how to use the weekend to recharge. For me, I like to just chill. My workload is heavy and exhausting, as I already shared, and the idea of having to go out and do something on the weekend doesn't make sense to me very often. [insert name here], on the other hand, really likes to use the weekends to go out and do something adventurous or spontaneous or at least go out and have some fun. I get it, but I just don't have the energy to do that.

We're a bit at odds right now and haven't figured out how to make it work. We usually compromise, but that means one of us usually not enjoying the time as much as the other partner. So, it creates that difficult thing, you know. We talked about alternating weekends, but I don't know if that makes sense.

But, yeah, other than this weekend issue, things seem to be going well. It would be interesting to hear what she has to say about that.

[few seconds pause]

Then there's my relationship with my daughter. With my daughter, I've noticed some distancing lately. I mean, we've had good connections, but she seems a bit disconnected now. Maybe it's me. Who knows. It's not bothering me too much; it just feels like usual pre-teenager angst. I'm happy, all things considered. She's an incredible human being. I don't deserve her. She makes me so proud. Her wit is wicked, guys. I love that about her. I guess she's just maturing and so there's some distancing or something like this, and I need to deal with this. I don't know.

I should probably go on about this a bit more, but I honestly don't have much more to say. Things are generally good.

[few seconds pause]

I have recently lost my father, as you know. Cancer. [pause] Sucks. I miss his smile. I miss our conversations. Life is short, isn't it? [chuckle] Well, you guys know that better than I do. It's crazy. One second, he's there, and you're carrying on minding your own business and doing the day-to-day things, taking it all for granted, and in the next second, or in our case, a few months, he's gone. You wonder if you said all the things you wanted to say. If you did everything you could do. If there was anything you could have said or asked about before it was too late.

Now I have, I don't know, like a gap in my life, a hole. You know? It's hard to make sense of it all.

[a few seconds pause]

I think it's appropriate now to shift to things that are holding me back. Obstacles. God, who doesn't have these right? You all probably know about some big obstacles I'll soon be facing, right? Yeah, so finances are one thing for me right now. Can't ever seem to get ahead. Work and work and work and there's just barely something there at the end of the month. If I had more money, I just, I guess, I don't know what I'd do. I feel like I'm not alone. At least in my circles, most people are struggling like I am. I'm sure there are some who are doing well. It feels like quicksand, though.

At least I have my health. I'm decently healthy. I take some meds for [insert minor medical condition], but that's not too big of a deal. I'm fortunate that my health isn't an obstacle.

[few seconds pause]

I guess my own attitude can be a problem sometimes. I can get a sort of "what's the point?" attitude. I suppose this could be an obstacle to things I want to accomplish. I know I have to have that drive. I just don't know where to get it from.

Work feels like a complete dead end, but I don't have the guts to exit my career and try something new. It's just too late in the game for that, it feels. It's too risky. I mean, my daughter needs me, and there's no sense in doing something like that right now.

There's the issue with my mother. She's not too happy about my recent life choices. We're in a good relationship with each other [...]. I guess I should have talked about her in my relationship section earlier [chuckle]. That's kind of odd that I didn't mention anything. I wonder what that says about my relationship with her. Funny [sigh]. Anyway, we're fine and we talk and all. It's just that ever-bearing-down look of disappointment that I've always got in the back of my mind. She wants me to be so much more. Not sure if that's an obstacle or not. I just feel like I'm always going to disappoint her or that I already have beyond repair. She's always saying, "River, I know there's more for you".

I don't think my partner is an obstacle. Like I shared earlier, she's good to me. We support each other. I feel that she has my back in whatever I choose to do. So, that's good.

Sometimes I wonder about moving, too. I feel stuck here in my work, but maybe in a similar position in a different company or a different place altogether might do the trick. I just can't help but wonder sometimes, you know. What if? What if a new place would help propel me and my family further?

[few seconds pause]

Overall, I'd say I'm doing okay. There's a feeling that I'm just floating along, though. I kind of wish there was more to me and what I'm doing. Maybe you all can share some insights about how I can level up some things in my life. But I'm mostly satisfied with how things are going, although I'm a bit lost in how to make life a bit more interesting. Things could be worse, so I'm grateful they aren't.

Anyway, that's about all I want to share. Those are my values right now and how things are going. What do you guys think?

~~~

Some thoughts before the next portion of the Hologram Conversation. Notice the subtle moments of introspection that do occur along the way. This process contains fits and starts. You will merge in and out of real-time reflection as you go. Feel free to indulge in these momentary reflections and then circle back to revisit a previous discussion point. Be flexible and thoughtful as you speak. You should not be judgmental at this point, even though River, in the sample, mentions a few regrets and wishes along the way. He implies that things are not perfect and should improve. However, he maintains positivity and continues despite these occasional negative thoughts. The point is to remain as carefree as possible and allow ideas and musings to flow.

Also, if any positive "aha" moments and personal realizations creep into the imaginary conversation, allow them to form. Those are valuable moments. The Hologram Conversation offers structure, but deviating from the structure for meaningful reflections and self-realizations is perfect. It only means the structure led you to these realizations and it is fulfilling its purpose.

Talking through your life via Hologram Conversations will illuminate many things, and you will be faced with sudden realizations that might shock you, both the beautiful and less desirable. Fully embrace this process and the depth of self-exploration you will achieve, even in step six alone.

Step 7 [Listening]

Once the sharing step is complete, you can rest in silence and "listen" to the replies from your holographic selves. This will take some imagination and concentration to see it through thoroughly. Obviously, no one is there to speak, so you will entertain this entire step in your mind. Everything will occur in your mind's eye. The perfection of this step in the Hologram Conversation takes some practice and time. Be patient with yourself. Because you are silent the entire time, the difficulty is remaining focused and not allowing your mind to wander.

For people with highly visual skills, this step may come easily. For others, this part will not only feel awkward but may also be challenging to execute as well.

Here are some recommended strategies. As mentioned in chapter four, taking notes can help. Opening your eyes can help; in this case, you can move your head around to "see" each person speaking from their space near you.

Maybe the opposite is true, and you need to close your eyes to remain focused.

Using hand gestures can really help, too. Offering verbal cues out loud can help. These can include words or phrases, such as: "yes," "mm-hmm," "uh-huh," "okay," "right," "really," "I understand," "interesting," "thank you," "wow," and "alright." These simple verbal cues, and many others, keep you attuned to the conversation. While this step should be primarily in silence, some verbalizations are appropriate. Staying verbally and audibly attached to the imaginary thoughts that will be shared by your future holographic selves helps ground you in the moment.

For this step, time spent will span anywhere from ten to thirty minutes. Listen to the thoughts of your future selves regarding some or all the things you shared from the previous step. You will not respond during this step unless you use verbal cues to stay connected to their thoughts.

As you listen, imagine their perspectives. Listen carefully to what they are saying, what they are appreciating, and what they are criticizing. They may even share with each other, disagreeing on some points or adding to each other's perspective. Listen with curiosity and intent, avoiding judgment or defensiveness. Remember, this is a golden opportunity to grow and learn. You are receiving "insider" information about yourself that should act as a guide moving forward. This process can be immensely intriguing to observe as your mind creates these future selves and makes them "speak."

When they finish speaking, thank them for their wisdom and their kindness to you. This will open you up for the next steps in the Hologram Conversation. It also helps you hold onto a positive frame of mind that is receptive to the breadth of feedback coming to you about your life.

Below is the continuation of this sample Hologram Conversation where the holographic selves begin responding.

The same disclaimers from step six apply here. These voices may sound cliché and unrealistic. We are working through a sample that contains a fictitious, hypothetical person with a hypothetical set of future selves. Remain focused on the model itself and remember that the specificity of your own life will provide the nuance and authenticity when you undergo the real thing.

[Look around and acknowledge each participant once again: a 40-year-old River, a 60-year-old River, and an 80-year-old River]

Forty-year-old: First of all, thank you for sharing your heart with us. Look, I'm quite proud of what you have going on right now. The fact that you've got a daughter who loves you and a partner who you appreciate and love despite some hiccups along the way is very fortunate. I look around and see so many of my friends, ones you will have in the future, who aren't so fortunate. They're struggling. Their relationships are faltering. Count yourself blessed and cherish this reality in your life fully.

Eighty-year-old: I agree. That you still have a range of relationships is something to cherish and to guard. Do the hard work to keep those in good standing. Sacrifice more time, even if you're tired. You can't afford to lose those people in your life. We can talk about the nuts and bolts of this later but finding a way to prioritize investments into your relationships, familial and beyond, I would say, is the most important thing you can work on right now.

Also, I wonder about your hobbies. You don't sound very excited, even about the one hobby you have right now. I wonder if you could give yourself a bit more time for your hobbies and possibly try a few more. Put yourself out there a bit. I know it's a time restraint issue. We'll work that part out together later. For now, I just want to share that maybe investing some time into a hobby would be a good idea and something that can bring rejuvenation against the backdrop of the strenuous parts of the day-to-day. I feel like you'll want some of that fulfillment from these side projects as life goes on. It doesn't get easier, you know. Life's ebbs and flows will bring more challenges; you'll see.

Forty-year-old: I also agree with the point about a hobby. Look, I'm in super grind mode right now. Think you've got it bad? I'm seeing my daughter's college years and its associated bills staring me down right now. I've been hustling to secure some more financial freedom for myself and my daughter. Things are tight and harder than ever. Everything is incredibly challenging. You need to find a way to wedge in some hobbies for your sanity's sake.

Sixty-year-old: I don't disagree with the others, but I think I have an additional perspective to contribute. I feel like you should think about your career a bit right now. You're at an age that's very important for solidifying your financial security for the long term. I feel like you should really think about either finding upward mobility in your current company, or maybe even moving out of your current town, as you had mentioned, or consider additional education and a shift in career. Yes, your current work pays the bills, but you are going to want a bit more financial security and maybe even a bit more satisfaction from your work as the years progress. This might be your last chance to make that happen. Once you hit your fifties, this is going to be too daunting a task to attempt. I'd say it's now or never on the career adjustment side of things and that this should take priority along with your relationships.

Eighty-year-old: Sure, that is a valid point. An audit or inventory of your current work and career path would be wise at this point. Devote some time to it. Invest it in. It may take some sacrifices, but it will be worth it in the future. You'll have a clearer sense of direction as well. Money can drive a lot of what you end up doing in life, for better or for worse. The clarity you will gain is good for you, and it helps you eventually focus your energy and attention on other things instead of constantly feeling anxious over your career.

Forty-year-old: On a side note, sorry to hear about your father, and mine for that matter. Time will help you cope, but take it from me, you will always miss him. I still do. You can't replace him, and you can't fill in the hole that is left behind.

Eighty-year-old: Yes, your father was special. He spoke many pearls of wisdom into you. You may not even realize just how profound he was yet. Try to remember his words of wisdom and use them as guidance.

Sixty-year-old: So, I know we just said career and relationships are very important, but I think we need to add another important thing. Regarding your health, you need to work on it right away. You'll have some health worries that creep up in your sixties. I'm all too familiar with this. You have time to make changes right now. Don't worry; it's not terminal, but it will diminish your quality of life a bit. So, find time to be more active; you will thank yourself later. And take a bit more care in your eating habits. It's the obvious thing for me to say, but it's also true. I'm living it right now, and it's not something to be taken lightly.

Forty-year-old: I suppose time management is something we should talk to you about. We're piling on even more demands when it seems you already feel overwhelmed and overworked right now.

Sixty-year-old: Yes, this is true.

Forty-year-old: You can see that there are many competing needs. If you take care of the time management thing first, then you can find more time for the competing priorities. For one thing, you might need to make some sacrifices regarding some things that gobble up your time. There's some waste that happens from time to time. Yes, you're tired from work, but channeling that energy into a hobby or exercise will rejuvenate you. Right now, the activities you default to don't recharge you or lift you up. They feel good at a dopamine level, but they aren't things that build sustainability and vitality over time; they take more than they give. It's time to rework the schedule so that you can fit in some of our suggestions. And it's time to take your values and priorities and use those as the motivation for removing the unnecessary things in your life right now.

Eighty-year-old: Back to the relationships, I'm so happy they are mostly strong. Challenges will be there, but that's normal. You don't need to have a huge collection of friends. Most will go away over time anyway, in one way or another. A sort of sifting the "wheat from the chaff" kind of process, if you know what I mean, is just fine. Just make sure to guard your best relationships and invest in them. You want a good handful of close friends who you know you can trust and who will be there for you in the hard times and you for them in their hard times. You want to be an asset to them, and they need to be an asset to you. This is the hallmark of good relationships.

You can constantly shuffle and add, or cut back, the more casual friends. This is especially true as you get older and some of your friends pass on. These casual friends are just friends on the periphery; they are there for mutual, casual enjoyment. Don't stress about having too many. Quality is better than quantity with these types. Just always keep your casual friends at arm's length. Don't share with them your personal victories or failures. Don't let them get too close; they don't deserve it. Reserve those personal parts of your life for those few close friends.

Sixty-year-old: Very true. I'm starting to already see the value of this in my life. Also, try to connect with friends who will help propel you forward in your activities and hobbies. Those can be good friends. Not the closest friends, but good friends. So many people I know have allowed their casual friends to drag themselves down. It doesn't have to be that way. If you find casual friends within your hobbies, those can be super rewarding friendships to have because they push you forward toward a more healthy and balanced life.

I'd also have some casual friends who can be good partners in business. These friendships allow you to share ideas, and sort of grow your skill sets through these partnerships. You might even find some business opportunities in the future with these friendships. I'd be actively seeking this out.

Eighty-year-old: I don't agree with this at all. Don't mix friendship with business endeavors. You will get burned. You'll figure this out eventually if you follow that advice. No, don't mix any business-related relationships with casual friendships. That's not going to work out well for you. I know what happens and it's not pretty.

Sixty-year-old: Not always. It's not always true. It depends on how you foster the relationships. You can have healthy, causal relationships within your work. I've seen it work. You can have these friends and avoid compromising situations.

Eighty-year-old: You are foolishly naïve to think you can mix these two. Don't worry, "60-year-old" self; you'll find out soon if you keep going down that pathway.

Forty-year-old: Well, we can agree to disagree and let him, over there, decide. I'd like to change the subject and comment on your busy schedule for a second. I don't find it that daunting, to be honest. You're fine. In fact, it sounds like you come home exhausted and unplug a bit. I agree that exercise and hobbies could be something to look forward to when you get home. However, the bedrock of joy and motivation at home is your partner and daughter. Don't let hobbies and exercise push these relationships to the background. If there's time for exercise, great; if not, then that's the way it goes. I'll be willing to discuss time management, of course, but I don't think you're as stuck as you think you are.

On a different note, I'd also like to add that I think you should have a serious talk with your daughter. I know we're going around in circles a bit in this conversation, but I've been thinking about what you said, and I feel we should address it. She is at an age where she can understand a straightforward conversation. I would sit down with her and discuss what you want to have out of your relationship with her. Tell her what you expect. Ask her to tell you the same, what she expects from you. Try to use this candid talk as a springboard into future discussions and toward a long-term healthy relationship.

Eighty-year-old: Yes, I agree. Maybe on the exercise and schedule part, you could alternate a bit, meaning some days could be exercise-focused and other hobbies-focused, and others could be family-focused. A good balance might help.

As for your daughter, I think what your "40-year-old" self said makes sense. But there are no lectures that work from the parent side. You should commit more to building your relationship with her through enjoyable experiences and activities that you create together. Be a bit intentional about it. Kids that age don't respond well to "sit down" talks. Actions definitely speak louder than words. Being intentional about spontaneous and fun activities could go a long way, too. It will take some work to figure out what she would really enjoy and appreciate, but it's possible. Talk to your partner about some ideas, as I think she knows your daughter well enough to offer some insight.

And while you're at it, it might be time to brainstorm a conversation you could have with your mother. Does she even know you feel the way you do? Maybe she's the way she is because this is her expression of love to you. I don't think you've had that sit-down with her. Instead of a sit-down with your daughter, it might be time for a sit-down with your mom. Share how you feel and do everything with assuming positive intentions and with a positive tone.

She and I had a very good relationship up to the day she passed on, so I would say there's hope for you in this.

Sixty-year-old: I like that. I like what you said, 80-year-old self. I want to go back to the exercise part you said. I would put exercise higher than some of the other things because it fuels everything else. You need to prioritize yourself at some point. If you're healthy, then you have more energy and the ability to meet all the additional demands on your time. I think prioritizing healthy eating and exercise will be the catalyst to success in so many other phases of your life.

Eighty-year-old: Fair enough. [turning to River] Look, I find that your overall direction in life is good. You seem to have some passive feelings and some defeated feelings. I, for one, can say that I'm damn proud of you. You have so much going for you. You got this. Just a few tweaks here or there, and you'll be humming along and even more satisfied with how your life is going.

I'm thinking that all you really need is some recentering of your direction in your career and some additional devotion to exercise, relationships, and hobbies. I know I just made it sound easy; it isn't. But this could do the trick to generate some renewed excitement in your life.

Forty-year-old: I agree.

Sixty-year-old: Yes, I think that's about it.

Eighty-year-old: Right, I think we've weighed in, briefly, on a few things. Now, it's time for us all to talk about this together. And so I now ask, "***What do "you" think about what we shared?***"

~~~

That is step seven of the Hologram Conversation. This sample illustrates what a brief commentary would look like by your future selves across the things you shared in step six. Step seven can go much longer with much more detail. In this sample, there are not, after all, many insights. The depth of this step is up to you. It can be the most rewarding step in the process if you want.

Remember, you can take notes during this time. Many clarifying ideas and directions in life can come to light in this step of the Hologram Conversation. If you wish to remember them, it might be beneficial to document them in writing. You can also have a method of audio recording so that you can avoid the distraction of writing. If your phone is supplying your audio recording source, then take extra care not to allow the phone to become a distraction in this process.

Now a brief note, again, about moving topic by topic through the Hologram conversation. While the argument to do it in the manner illustrated helps you share everything you need to share without interruption, it can also be possible to break up the sharing topic by topic. Organizationally, it would mean you would rotate between steps six and seven across each of the major talking points (values, busy aspects of life, relationships, and obstacles). It would be several cycles you would complete across steps six and seven. This is possible, but you must remain focused.

These two steps were not the back and forth just yet; they were you sharing without disruption and then your holographic selves sharing back without disruption. If you hold to this process strictly, then a topic-by-topic cycle is possible.

Step 8 [Dialogue]

The final step of the Hologram Conversation is the ever-important dialogue portion of the process. This will be the step that feels the most like a natural conversation. All the heavy lifting in preparation for this stage serves to ensure this part is particularly rich, encouraging, and insightful. You can now proceed into an imaginative conversation that should prove to be transformative. Below is a sample dialogue. Obviously, a normal and natural dialogue will ebb and flow in ways no sample could ever predict.

As mentioned before, this continues to be a hypothetical, fictitious character with hypothetical, fictitious future selves. Ignore the cliché in the sample provided. Rather, focus on the model. Furthermore, the following model is not a prescribed template. It is only what it purports to be: a sample that serves as a reference point. This sample provides the "spirit" of the process and gives you a sense of what you should be doing with the dialogue step of the Hologram Conversation.

[Look around again and acknowledge each participant: a 40-year-old River, a 60-year-old River, and an 80-year-old River]

You: Alright, I'd like to start by discussing my relationship with my daughter. I hear what you're saying, but I'm a bit curious. How do you see me doing this successfully? It's ideal, of course, to build that relationship. Whether it's a sit-down or through some experiences, she's a tough one to crack. I just don't see it working out where she wants to go do something with her "old, out of touch" dad. I can visualize her eyes rolling to the back of her head. What do you guys suggest to sort of break through this barrier of parent-to-child challenges in the teenage years?

Sixty-year-old: River, you've got a few precious years left to make a final, lasting imprint. She may not be fully receptive right now. She may ignore you. But she'll come to you when you're about 60 years old and say that she regretted spending so little quality time with you in high school. She will admit that even if she wouldn't have listened, she wished that you had made a stronger effort to be in her life. So, I say reach out regardless of how she reacts. Insist on spending time with her. Just find places where she won't be seen by her peers. Seek advice from other parents. Use the internet to find ideas. Find a support group online that can help you. If all those ideas sound too overwhelming, then just be yourself and open up to her about what you want to see develop in your relationship with her. I can confirm that she wanted you there with her all along, even though she communicated the seemingly opposite. Persistence.

What do you think, 80-year-old self?

Eighty-year-old: I agree in principle. But I think you need to be cautious as well. This whole approach may feel very forced and cause further distancing between you two. Handle this conversation carefully and over time. That's why I recommended reaching out more subtly through experiences or common interests.

What additional insights I can offer is that I do know that we've grown cold again in my later years, my daughter and me. I'm not exactly sure why. So, proceed with caution. Really think about the long-term connections that you want to establish. Think how you want to relate to her when you're my age. Try to plant the seeds for that now, even if it feels like she doesn't hear you.

You: Interesting. Hmm. How would I do this? I mean, I try to connect with her. I'm a bit worried about doing a whole transparent approach with her. I'm just not sure the ideas you all have offered would work. I have no idea what shared experience we could have. Yes, I can scour the internet and check in with other parents. But it's definitely uncool to "hang with dad" right now. I don't see how I'm getting past this part.

Forty-year-old: Well, I can tell you that some things I'm doing right now are working. We're doing monthly father-daughter dates. She chooses the place, and we agree upon a time. It's worked so far. I wish I had started them sooner. She really appreciates it, especially as she's launching her career and is more open to advice now. I don't know if my approach makes any sense, but at least we are talking again and in a meaningful way.

Also, at her age, I bet a movie theater in the neighboring town, so that she won't be embarrassed around her friends, would work. Her tastes can't be so bad in movies. Surely there would be something you could go see with her that you'd both enjoy. Movies aren't exactly quality time, but afterward, you could go out for dessert, and then you'd have your chance to speak with her and build that relationship back up.

You: Okay, so regular father-daughter dates with her deciding where we go, and some theatre nights might work. Anything else?

Sixty-year-old: You need to listen. You're so busy and, at the same time, a bit lethargic about life, and she feels that. She senses the angst you have and the giving-in kind of attitude. You shouldn't hide your feelings from her, but she definitely needs to know you're present and can be there for her. I mean, don't dump your baggage onto her, but sharing a few summarizing statements about how you're human just like everyone else and that you're trying to find your way in life could be quite inspirational to her.

I don't think she'd see you as weak. She'd see you as being real about life. She thinks a ton of things are terrible too. She would be able to relate. Of course, the danger would be to make this all about you. That's why I suggest a few statements and then move on to asking her about how she's trying to find her way in her own situations. Find some way to show her that you're there and aware of her own challenges, not just consumed by your own.

You: Thank you [pause]. Thank you for that. I'll have to think about this for a while. You've given me some ideas to work with, I think.

[few seconds pause]

So, what about my career? Eighty-year-old self, you seem to want me to tap more into my hobbies. You know I don't have time for this. I need to get my career solidified or changed like the others have suggested.

How can I possibly find the time or motivation to add those to my schedule right now? In fact, all of you have hinted at my schedule. I can't just invent more hours in the day. Reality is what it is. I'm stuck. What do you all say to this?

Eighty-year-old: River, in the end, you don't get any badges for working your life away. You also don't get any badges for binge-watching movies. Nor do you get any for drinking away the frustrations. There is time outside of work; it exists. You need to be more intentional about it. Look, I get it, you do need to take care of your career, I know. That is important. It's not unimportant. But so is your health and your family and your friends. I don't know what to say other than this is the great juggle everyone faces in modern society. You'll have to make sacrifices and say "no" to some things. You have to reshuffle some priorities a bit. That's it.

I just wish I had said "no" far more often. Given what you've shared with us today, I think you might need to say "no" to this company and find a company that will provide you the flexibility you need to hold your boundaries and put your family above your work. Yes, I know, not easy! In this market, it will take a lion's effort. The question is whether it will pay off in the end. And it won't happen overnight, and neither will it happen if you take no action. Small actionable steps each day. Start a search. Poke around a bit. See what's out there. Get curious. Make some steps each day. I mean, or not. You can just sit there where you are and not make any changes. That's the alternative. You're free to do as you please.

Or, as others have said, you could seek out opportunities within the company you currently work with that will serve you better. You say there seems to be no upward mobility, but are you sure? Have you knocked on that door yet? You'll spend decades at the end so frustrated, and even angry, that you didn't make the move earlier on in life if you stand still and do nothing. You'll also justify your inaction to yourself through the years, saying it just wouldn't have worked out anyway, or that it wasn't meant to be, or that everything just happens for a reason. Either the frustration or the justifications will take over throughout the years if you don't take action.

As for the hobbies, I stand by what I've shared. You need them. It doesn't matter how tired you are or how insignificant they seem. The device in your hands at night is what's insignificant. The television at night is what's insignificant. It's just about priorities and being disciplined. I'm being harsh right now, sure. I understand. However, what you need to understand is that pushing yourself just a bit more to be disciplined with your time will reap serious benefits. It will be one of the best decisions you've ever made to make hobbies a greater part of your life.

You: Yeah, much easier said than done. Sounds a bit like wishful thinking, to be honest. I'm too exhausted to even think about a hobby after work most days. So, I'm not sure what to do with your advice, to be honest.

Forty-year-old: Look, look, there are opportunities. You just need to hustle right now. You owe it to yourself and your daughter and to your partner. I'm doing it now, and it's working. New company, new learning curves, new challenges, and all that it entails. However, now I have more opportunities with my daughter. It's within your grasp, even if it feels like it isn't.

I've even found some time for some side things. For me, it's golf right now. I get in a few holes each week. It's a huge stress relief. I've met a few friends out on the greens. It's been worth it. It's hard to make the time work, but worth it. Chin up, man. Don't wallow in pity or act self-defeated. Like we said, what's the alternative? Giving in will only spiral you down further. Every day should be your fight for better things, a standing defiance against all the odds that push against you.

Sixty-year-old: I'm not so much in agreement with this advice. I mean, if you are stretched thin already, adding more family time, more hobbies, more career advancement, and more friend devotion will simply derail you. There's no path toward success if you do it all at once.

Slow down. Pick one thing for this month that you'll target. Once you can handle it, maybe next month or the month after, you can add on one more thing. All this advice should be taken, evaluated, and sorted by priority. You are only human and can only do so much, especially when you're already overwhelmed.

Maybe you start with yourself. What if you started by working on your health and exercise first? Maybe that would be rewarding enough as you'd see positive changes in yourself, all while adding stamina to handle the next few things you're going to add to your plate later.

You: Got it. I hear you all. I'll have to think about this and make some decisions. Thank you for giving me insight. I think starting with my health first might be a good idea as it might give me the boost to venture into other values and improve them after some time. I think I'll look up some time management strategies and read up a bit to see how I can make some small changes right away.

[few seconds pause]

Alright, I've got a bit more time to explore a few more points. What about my romantic relationship? Any advice?

Forty-year-old: I must admit that I'm lonely right now. I have those few close friends I was telling you about. They are a godsend. However, a romantic partner is something I have lost at this stage of life. I went full-on career mode and alienated my partner.

This kind of loneliness that I feel right now will eat at you. It's worse than I thought it would be. I see so many people supposedly happy being alone right now. I thought their path could be mine. I don't understand how their public-facing self is so happy. Nothing could be further from the truth for me.

I swear to you, you must work on yourself and in doing so make sure you have, or need to go find, a compatible partner.

You won't want to rely on your daughter to vent your feelings because you know that using her as an emotional crutch as she grows into adulthood is unfair. You have to take care of yourself. You'd become a burden to her. She has her own family now, and she has huge responsibilities with them. You can't add your own insecurities and personal messes to her responsibilities.

You should seek a viable partner in life; it's worth it to do life and share life with someone else. For your health, for your sanity, and for the simple reason that life is difficult, and it's helpful doing it with a partner.

Eighty-year-old: Yes, and there's no perfect partner. There's a whole massive crowd of potential "someones" you could do life with and do just fine. You're already with a partner. If things are okay, then proceed and develop that relationship. If it ends up being someone else, then fine. Just seek friendships and make sure they stay healthy, lifting you and your partner up in life.

Sixty-year-old: This is the ideal that your 80-year-old self is sharing, and I agree that you'll need to chase it. You may fall short. But you must at least strive for it. Your 80-year-old self is right. Seeking companionship is the smartest path forward. What's that quote about better to have loved and failed than to never have loved? I'm seeing the writing on the wall for me. It's starting to feel a bit too late right now as well. My path was the one of your 40-year-old self, and I've been stuck for years. Twenty years of doing my own thing, yes, and it's been a good ride, yes, but life that isn't shared with someone close is a lonely life for sure. I mean, that's just my opinion.

I've had plenty of friends to share experiences with, but it's not the same as an intimate relationship. You know, the downs and the ups. You need someone to mourn with, to cheer with, to laugh with, to love with. Life loses so many of its colors without good relationships, not just the romantic ones. It's worth fighting for, even if you never find it. The good news for you is that you might have found your partner. Now cultivate it. Hold it. Invest in it. And if it doesn't work out, then keep fighting to find a partner who will fit with you.

Eighty-year-old: Yes, that is the essence of what I was trying to share. Better to try than not at all.

You: Thank you for that advice. Yes, today's romantic world seems to be insanely confusing. I'm concerned for my daughter, too.

Anyway, thank you for the encouragement to fight for this. I think that's the spirit that's needed in my life right now.

Forty-year-old: I think what we're getting at is that we can't help you with this stuff other than offer what we're experiencing right now and what we're feeling. We can't know if your current partner is a good fit. Only you can know this by leaning into the relationship to be sure. Another thing to consider is to discuss your values with your current partner. You can confirm if there's alignment or not by doing this.

I'm wondering about your platonic relationships. Let's discuss those a bit.

[few seconds pause]

You: No. I'm sorry. It's a lot to take in right now. I'd rather postpone any talk about my life's values and priorities until next time.

In terms of romantic relationships, thank you. It makes sense.

[few seconds pause]

I think I would like to talk about one more thing, though. We never actually discussed my values. What do think about my values?

Sixty-year-old: Ah yes, we forgot to start with those. I like them. They make sense to me. I mean, you don't seem to have anything out of balance or out of the ordinary. I wonder if you really believe in each of them, though. When you first shared, you seemed a bit nonchalant and noncommittal.

I feel like values are something you find nonnegotiable in life. They are what you fight for. Do you have that fire in your belly about them? Or are you just listing these because you think these are the typical values that someone who is a good person in society would embrace? If it's the latter, then I suggest you do some soul-searching and rethink your values a bit more. You can cut back. You can add. You can keep everything the same. Just be sure you're fully committed to them.

Overall, though, I think we all agree that what you've shared makes sense and has value so long as you're committed to them.

Eighty-year-old: I think they are fine. They seem a bit narrow. What other values might you have? Do you value anything fun? Or creative? Maybe you value building new skills? Maybe you could look into something related to art or design? I wonder about building life-long relationships being a value. I wonder if making beautiful memories could be a value worth identifying. Maybe some specificity could help drive you forward in your life.

You: Stop.

[few seconds pause]

Let me just process everything for a few minutes. I'm starting to feel overwhelmed, and I don't want to get to that point in my conversations with you guys.

[few minutes pause]

Thank you. Thank you, each of you, for all the things you've shared with me in this conversation. I think I'm going to end the conversation at this point.

After everything we've discussed, here's where I'm at: I feel like with my career concerns, I can figure it out; that's doable. The hobbies thing I feel like I can work on that too. I just need to figure out some time management strategies and use my evenings more purposefully to gain energy instead of allowing any remaining energy to be sucked out of me. I think you all are right, and that focus on my health can, and should, be my first priority.

I still feel a bit unclear about the relationships, but we can explore this in more detail next time.

Next time, I want to know more about the positive directions you've taken and how I can follow your advice in that way. There were a lot of warnings and regrets in today's conversation.

Eighty-year-old: Maybe reach out to real people in your life who you trust on some of the topics we discussed today to get a bit more insight. Remember, we are you. We are only your mind. However, at the same time, we know you the best because we are you. Others are not you. Take others' views with some caution. Their motives aren't always the best.

[few seconds pause]

You: Fair enough.

Sixty-year-old: We aren't trying to attack you. We care about you. We want you to become more than what we became.

You: Of course, of course, yes, I know. I understand. I appreciate everything. I'll find a way. Look, I'm exhausted. Let me have a think on this and return to our conversation at a later time.

All holographic selves: You're welcome. Goodbye.

~~~

This Hologram Conversation can last much longer or much shorter. You may choose to make the entire conversation about a singular decision as opposed to a whole life's survey and exploration. You may notice, even in the provided sample, that not all talking points were discussed during the dialogue section. What you cover is up to you.

It will take some creativity and imagination. If you pull it off, however, you will start gaining incredible insights and leverage that inner voice for something productive and meaningful. Hologram Conversations can rudder your life.

To commit to this process requires extensive work, commitment, and focus. It can be too much to take in all at once. Feel free to try shortened sessions as needed and home in on one or two values or priorities. It is not necessary to change your entire life in one session.

For example, you could look at just relationships with one session. Or look at finances alone. Or focus on a big, pending decision. You are the driver of the process, so you get to decide what matters to you in these discussions. The samples are mere frameworks.

While this chapter provided a sample, which made it quite long, it should provide a helpful level of specificity to a Hologram Conversation.

Chapter 6:

Putting It All Together

Leverage your inner voice; rudder your life. -Joshua Smalley

While what you do during a Hologram Conversation establishes everything, what you do after a Hologram Conversation is equally important. The challenge is to have Hologram Conversations inspire, influence, and challenge you. Unlike New Year's Resolutions, where it is easy to walk away unchanged after a week's time, the conversations from this book have the potential to stay powerful and have a transformational impact. Everything hinges on the time that follows a Hologram Conversation.

The first thing to do is take a break. Given how intense and potentially exhausting the process of the Hologram Conversation may have been, it would be good to pause for a short while. You could go on a short walk, hydrate, stand and stretch, meditate, create art, ride a bicycle, or play instrumental music. Whatever you enjoy, take some time to indulge in it as you reflect on the conversation.

Do something relaxing that pulls you out of the Hologram Conversation but not too far away from it. For example, watching a movie or going to an event immediately following a Hologram Conversation is a bad idea. You need to be in a relaxing and reflective headspace to absorb what was shared. Moving immediately to an entirely different experience or event that may distract you defeats the purpose of the conversation.

For me, I usually need about five minutes to experience a reflective reset. Sometimes, I need longer. Each person will need their own break in their own time frame. This reset is similar to when you smell too many perfumes consecutively and need to reset your olfactory system. Often, people smell coffee beans as a break from the powerful smells of perfumes. Consider this quick break after the Hologram Conversation as a coffee bean-smelling break for your mind.

Next, you should document the main takeaways from the conversation. Now, some individuals might prefer to journal during or immediately after the conversation so as not to forget anything. If this method works for you, and you do not need the extra rest, that's wonderful.

As for journaling itself, there is no shortage of journals, journaling methods, and reflection protocols easily found on the internet. Use what is most comfortable for you. If you do not have a journaling method, then it would be wise to conduct a bit of research on an appropriate journaling method for you before beginning a Hologram Conversation.

Also, feel freedom in your method of journaling. You can use audio recordings, video recordings, a speech-to-text application, typing on a word processor, the old-fashioned pen and paper style, or any other style appropriate to the task.

The value of documentation might be intuitive but can be described on many levels. First, it is a rudimentary method to **keep track of the conversations** you have held over time. What were the takeaways? What are the big ideas that keep coming up in the conversations? Being able to go back and review is a beneficial practice that validates and establishes the value of Hologram Conversations in your life.

Somewhat related to tracking the conversations is the sense that you can **create a long-term narrative of your journey** through journaling. This is a more macro view of the conversations through journaling. This second value behind journaling can provide the story of who you are and where you are going over time across many Hologram Conversations. You can observe and monitor your evolution, growth, and maturation that comes from these conversations.

Third, journaling after Hologram Conversations provides **accountability**. As humans, we all need various methods of accountability to help keep ourselves on track. In times when we fail to hold ourselves accountable, we realize the need for such a system. Whatever your method of journaling, it will provide a means to maintain consistency and success over time, holding yourself to a high standard and maximizing the potential of Hologram Conversations.

Fourth, journaling provides a clear **pathway forward**. Journaling provides the blueprints for the next steps. For those who feel that Hologram Conversations are worth trying but are, nevertheless, a bit abstract, journaling narrows in on the pragmatic, systematic, and clear steps for implementation. If all the zany imagination and in-your-head world of Hologram Conversations, journaling puts something practical in your hands—the ideas you will commit to because of this unique process. As such, journaling helps those unnerved by the abstract nature of these conversations take comfort in the potential utility and meaningfulness of the entire process.

Fifth, you can use journaling as an **evaluation tool**. Are Hologram Conversations worth it? If not, why not? Can some aspects of the process be redeemed and adapted? If it is working, what are the real changes? Have you made decisions as a result of Hologram Conversations that have led to positive changes? Are you coming to profound realizations about yourself? Journaling can make it explicitly clear whether this process is beneficial or not.

A Note About Hologram Conversation Timings

When should you conduct these conversations?

This process can be done periodically in life. On the other hand, it can also be done more regularly if you find value in regular self-check-ins. As previously noted, it can also be initiated due to an important pending decision.

Avoid the cliché timings. The New Year's Resolution types of life resets are too easily ignored. Leave your New Year's Resolutions in their place and time and let them function as they always do for you, whether successful or not. Hologram Conversations are a far more intentional and intensive process than an annual New Year's wish list. Intentionally design your Hologram Conversations around important times in your life.

That said, if you are a systems person, you could do something like quarterly, annually, semi-annually, or monthly Hologram Conversations. Creating intervals of time for these conversations can create accountability due to their scheduled regularity. If arranging these conversations in purposeful time frames makes sense to you, wonderful. Put it in the calendar and then rest at ease that you have a plan moving forward.

You could also set your Hologram Conversations just before significant decisions in life. Do you have a job or career shift pending? Do you have a relationship moving into serious territory, and you want to know what your next steps should be? Are you about to make a huge purchase? Are you about to move to a new town or country? Are you about to make an addition to your family? Are you about to learn new skills? Are you about to start school? Are you about to exit school? Are you about to take on a serious challenge? Have you recently gone through serious loss or trauma? Are you worried about something coming up in life—a medical procedure, a confrontation, a risky task? All these scenarios, and more, are appropriate life milestones that may initiate a Hologram Conversation.

Seeking wisdom from your future selves around such important matters before you are bombarded with the sometimes-confusing advice of well-intentioned outside voices (family, friends, online, doctors, specialists, etc.) is a wise idea. Prioritize seeking to understand yourself before letting the other voices into your life. Be the guardian and platformer of your inner voice.

You could also set your Hologram Conversations around questions you want answered in life. Maybe your first session is about self-discovery. You could lead with, "Who am I?" Maybe your next question could be, "Who do I want to be?" or "Why do I always do [insert behavior here]?" and so on and so forth.

If you intend to make changes in your life, Hologram Conversation may aid in this process. Maybe you want to break a habit or do some personal work. You can narrow in on the goals and aspirations for these changes you wish to make in your life. You can ground this enormous challenge of self-change upon a Hologram Conversation.

These previous three reasons (life decisions, questions, and changes) for conducting Hologram Conversations help narrow the focus of the process. They may be more intense and truncated as the attention rests upon a singular point instead of a full-life survey.

You could also set your Hologram Conversations to strategically evaluate or interrupt the routines and ruts of your life. Maybe you feel like life is wasting away or maybe life feels like it is being taken for granted. Or maybe things are going along the status quo, and you wonder if there is more to life than a roboticized pathway. Maybe you feel too settled and you want a bit more adventure. This angst might be a strong motivator for these conversations.

Maybe life is the opposite; it's too chaotic, and you're seeking clarity, calm, and peace. In this case, a Hologram Conversation might act as the self-therapy you so desperately need.

All these reasons, and more, are appropriate catalysts for Hologram Conversations.

~~~

Addressing Potential Concerns

How do you work around simply "saying what's expected"? How do you expand beyond the predicted responses? How do you avoid cliché? You might be thinking that all you will "hear" in these conversations is, "Hey, be nicer to people and tell those closest to you that you love them. Oh, and gosh darn it, stop that annoying habit. And save some money. And smile and have fun in life, you." You can imagine the finger-wagging parental condescension with every statement. What can be done to avoid this?

The answer? The answer is as cliché as it gets: be true to yourself. This does not mean automatically taking on the opposite of societal norms to feel authentic. So many, it seems, see societal norms and respond dualistically, either giving in or running the opposite way. Are not both these responses mere reactions and inauthentic to us as individuals? Are we not nuanced people with a range of realities that both comport with and deviate from societal norms?

As a result, your authentic Hologram Conversations will likely be a blend of the stereotypical along with the idiosyncrasies that comprise you.

Find your real self, the one whose values do not need to impress, be recognized, or win any awards. Your real values do not need external validation on social media or in dinner conversations. The real values you hold may be apolitical, areligious, and not dictated by social construction alone. The real you holds values independent of the pressures around you. In a sequel to this book, I will detail a process for exploring and identifying these values and then mapping them into your life.

What if This Process Fails?

This is an excellent question. There are many possible responses. One response is to try it a few more times in case success is more about incremental changes occurring over time rather than radical, immediate change.

Another response could be to examine yourself in every step—did you fully commit to each step without disruptions? A self-analysis might help you find a gap in the process previously undetected.

Another response might be to overhaul the process to something that would be better aligned with your own way of doing things. Maybe you need to take the model from this book and make significant changes to make it work for you.

Another response would be to shorten the actual conversation. Sometimes, the model tries to bite off too much. It might also be the case that you need to persevere for a while; trying something new at the beginning may not feel successful, and it may take practice and skill-building to eventually reach competence in something new.

Yet another response might be that it will not work for you. It may be the case that Hologram Conversations cannot meet the needs of every person.

What if I Get Answers I Do Not Like?

Do you want to seek truth in your life? Then, proceed no matter how risky and uncomfortable it may feel. Consider conducting a follow-up conversation, asking your future selves to elaborate for greater clarity. Why are these answers disconnected from what you expect?

Ultimately, you may need to face inconvenient realities about yourself that emerge from these conversations. If answers end up being particularly negative, consider seeking a mental health professional to investigate further.

What if the answers are too radical and could dramatically impact my life? Should I really listen?

If your imagination seems to have taken a wild ride, and ideas from the Hologram Conversations ask you to sell everything and move to a remote island, it might be time to talk to others and seek additional advice. Talk to your family and friends, the closest ones to you, who have your best in mind. Seek the opinion of experts. Maybe conduct another Hologram Conversation and ask your future selves why they would encourage you in such a radical direction. Be cautious. Hologram Conversations cannot be the sole reason to randomly embark on an illogical pathway in life.

What if my future holographic selves say nothing?

This is possible. Stay in silence and listen. If they say nothing, then you know even your imagination does not have a path forward regarding the topic you are exploring. Simply put that topic on pause and revisit it at another time. Sometimes, there are no responses to life's complexities.

What if I'm Not a Visual Person?

Find ways to make the process more concrete and pragmatic. I have offered suggestions, but your own self-knowledge will problem-solve more effectively than anyone else. To reiterate some suggestions, always have a notebook. Use physical objects to stand in for future holographic selves, such as picture frames or large pillows placed around you. Keep your eyes open and narrate each step you are taking to make it feel more deliberate and clinical. Everyone needs different things. Be a self-advocate and find a way to overcome obstacles as opposed to ditching the entire process altogether. You may never know what you are missing if you abandon Hologram Conversations.

Final Words

Movements addressing mental health and promoting positive self-talk gurus are everywhere, and the research is becoming more apparent than ever. With that backdrop, this book provides a practical process for participating in self-talk that is intentional and transformational. This process can be considered many things: a ritual, a model, a framework, a system, a guide, and a way of living. If you want to intentionally manage your inner voice and use it to do the hard work of self-awareness, exploration, and growth, then Hologram Conversations are a useful tool. This process is about leveraging that inner voice that exists inside of you.

I recommend that you do not share your venture into Hologram Conversations with others until you have worked on it for a while and seen its benefits in your life. It is a bit of an odd process and difficult to describe. Most people will look at you like they looked at me when I first began sharing the process. Their left eyebrow would rise in skepticism. With time, those most skeptical have tried this method with me and have shared how beautiful the process became for them.

Also, not everyone has your best interest in mind and will find any excuse to keep you from becoming your best self. Some may sabotage your attempt with these conversations due to their initial reaction to the oddity of it all. If you undergo the process first, then you can let the evidence of its benefits drive you forward into genuine sharing opportunities with others.

Through Hologram Conversations, you can continue the difficult work of being your best in the world. You can take back control over your inner dialogues. You can more clearly manage the voices in your mind and who gets to share in these conversations. It is time we rudder our lives more intentionally.

Let the inner voice revolution begin in you.

~~~

I Value You

Dear Reader,

Thank you for joining us in the Hologram Conversation journey. I hope that engaging in the Hologram Conversation process proves to be a significant experience for you. The beauty of these conversations is that you can customize each step to your needs. I trust you have begun leveraging your inner voice to navigate life's challenges, grow as a person, and solidify your personal values.

If what you encountered in this book has resonated with you, then I would greatly appreciate your honest feedback. What you share will help readers know if this is the right book for them. It can highlight the importance of this book for people's lives. More importantly, it helps make this book more visible and accessible to people around the world.

If this book has made an impact on you, then it will likely impact others as well. Your partnership in this is invaluable.

Here is how you can provide your valuable feedback:

You can leave a review, detailed or brief, on Amazon, Audible, or Goodreads.

Here are some questions to consider when composing a review:

- **Is this book helping you be more intentional with your inner voice?**
- **Is this book helping you navigate difficult decisions more effectively?**
- **Is this book inspiring personal growth?**
- **Is this book helping you solidify your personal values?**
- **Is this book helping you understand yourself better?**

With these questions in mind, you can steer readers to the potential impact this book has to offer.

Thank you once again for your support. I look forward to reading your thoughts!

Sincerely,

Joshua Smalley

Feel free to reach out directly to me via either of these two points of contact:

hologramconversations@gmail.com

www.youtube.com/travelingteachr

References

Gandhi, M. (n.d.). *Mahatma Gandhi quotes.* https://quotefancy.com/quote/856327/Mahatma-Gandhi-Everyone-who-wills-can-hear-the-inner-voice-It-is-within-everyone

Lamontagne, R. (n.d.). *Ray Lamontagne quotes.* https://www.brainyquote.com/quotes/ray_lamontagne_497477

Monk, M. (n.d.). *Meredith Monk quotes.* https://www.brainyquote.com/quotes/meredith_monk_213174

Rahman, A. R. (n.d.) *A. R. Rahman quotes.* https://www.brainyquote.com/quotes/a_r_rahman_623296

Winfrey, O. (n.d.). *Oprah Winfrey quotes.* https://www.azquotes.com/quote/1250317?ref=inner-voice